A NEW VIEW OF CONGREVE'S
WAY OF THE WORLD

UNIVERSITY OF MICHIGAN
CONTRIBUTIONS IN MODERN PHILOLOGY
NUMBER 23

A NEW VIEW OF
CONGREVE'S
WAY OF THE WORLD

by

PAUL AND MIRIAM MUESCHKE

ANN ARBOR
THE UNIVERSITY OF MICHIGAN PRESS

1958
Library of Congress Catalog Card No. 57-9136

ACKNOWLEDGMENTS

We are grateful to the trustees of the Horace H. Rackham School of Graduate Studies for a research grant, and to Professors Louis I. Bredvold and Oscar James Campbell for stimulating comments on our manuscript.

PRINTED IN THE NETHERLANDS
BY N.V. DRUKKERIJ G. J. THIEME, NIJMEGEN

A NEW VIEW OF CONGREVE'S
WAY OF THE WORLD

Most critics agree that *The Way of The World* is the masterpiece of Restoration comedy. Aside from agreement on this point, criticism of this comedy has been and still is impressionistic, fragmentary, and contradictory. Ever since Jeremy Collier stigmatized Restoration comedy with the charges of irreverence and immorality, critics have tended to examine the genre in a gingerly manner.

There are two major approaches to Restoration comedy, the aesthetic and the moral. Critics favoring an aesthetic approach frequently evade the moral issue by praising perfection of style and disregarding thought; the extremists in this group not only shear sound from sense, but also imply that Congreve himself has set a precedent for so doing since "wit was really his be-all and his end-all."[1] Critics disturbed by the alleged immorality of Restoration comedy grant lip service to the pre-eminence of this comedy in its genre, then proceed to attack the merit of the genre and the worth of the comedy regarded as the culmination of the genre. Both groups of critics continue to assert that *The Way of the World* is a masterpiece, but neither assembles much evidence to substantiate the assertion. Frequently, instead of showing why this play is a masterpiece, critics seem bent on proving that by all acceptable criteria, it could not possibly be one. Either perplexed by or distrustful of the genre itself, as well as by the master creation of the genre, critics commenting on *The Way of the World*, at times condemn, at times condone: the immorality, the cynical tone, the tangled plot, the witty lovers, the unflagging brilliance and wit of the dialogue, and the artificial nature of the surprise in the denouement.

Allardyce Nicoll,[2] most influential and most quoted of living Restoration critics, in attempting to reconcile the conflicting points of view of his predecessors and contemporaries, reaches these bewildering conclusions:

"This comedy of manners is a peculiar, intangible sort of thing. ... when we say that Congreve's comedy is a comedy of manners we are using the word in its Congrevian sense, betokening something brilliant about a man or a woman, not a humour, but a grace ... something that 'looks a little *Jene-scay-quoysh*' [sic]" (p. 184), "... it is difficult to hazard even an indistinct definition of the type. ... the invariable elements ... [are] at least one pair of witty lovers ... their dialogue free and graceful, an air of refined cynicism over the whole production, the plot of less consequence than the wit ... [There is] a total lack of any emotion whatsoever. ..." (pp. 184–185). "That the Congrevian comedy was immoral, no one can deny, unless by a species of sophism not unknown to modern critics. ..." (p. 186). "There is no sentiment in it [*The Way of the World*], no realism, no coarseness. Mirabell and Millamant, about whom the plot, such as it is, gyrates continually, are not complete figures: they are merely automata, devised as mouth-pieces for the poet. The theme is artificial and the conclusion is artificial ... yet both have a brilliancy and a truth which make of *The Way of the World* the master-creation of the school of manners" (p. 231).

If we accept Nicoll as mentor, and many scholars still do, we are confronted with a mythical masterpiece the merit of which we must accept on faith. He implies that an artificial theme and an artificial conclusion are somehow transmuted into brilliancy and truth; yet he states neither the theme nor the truth. Furthermore, he presents an amazing array of negations which somehow coalesce into the "master creation of the school of manners." It is: "intangible"; "has no sentiment"; "no emotion"; "no passion"; "no coarseness"; "no realism"; "no morality"; "the plot is of less consequence than wit"; Mirabell and Millamant are "automata"; their charm is "*Jen-scay-quoysh*"; the theme and the conclusion are "artificial"—we must conclude that Congreve's famed comedy, if it be a masterpiece, is the "master creation" of truth and brilliancy *in vacuo*.

The aim of this essay is to determine why, despite the dissensions of the critics and the mutations of taste and time, *The Way of the World* has survived, and deserves to survive, as the masterpiece of Restoration comedy.

We propose to show that it is the insight with which the progressive regeneration of one pair of adulterers is contrasted with the progressive degeneration of another pair of adulterers; that it is the artistry with which the balanced and antithetical form of wit is repeated in the balanced and antithetical intrigue and counterintrigue; that it is the ingenuity with which plot, character, and dialogue are integrated with the exposure of adultery; and that above all else, it is the depth, variety, and subtlety of the wit emanating from the repudiation of *carpe diem* philosophy which establishes the eminence of *The Way of the World* in the satiric tradition of Horace and Ben Jonson.

To establish our point of view we begin with a number of assumptions diametrically opposed to those now generally accepted: (1) that the plot is primarily a legacy conflict centering in Lady Wishfort and the four adulterers; (2) that the theme is the danger of losing "fame and fortune" through the exposure of adultery; (3) that the title is an oblique thrust at evils inherent in the contemporary marriage of convenience; (4) that the stock character types (the rake, the cast [off] mistress, the adultress, the cuckold, and the irresponsible guardian) hitherto usually regarded as embodiments of folly, are deliberately modified to reveal how unchecked folly degenerates into vice; (5) and finally, that the epigrammatic, antithetical form of wit formerly associated with the ridicule of folly is taxed with a dual function, sometimes to ridicule folly, other times to expose vice.

The theme appears on the title page of this play,[3] explicit in two quotations from Horace:

Audire est operæ pretium, procedere recte
Qui mæchis non vultis—Horat. Lib. i. Sat. 2.
[Ye that do not wish well to the proceedings of adulterers, it is worth your while to hear how they are hampered on all sides.]

Metuat, doti deprensa.—*Ibid.*
[The woman fears for her dowry, if she should be caught.]

The theme is reiterated and emphasized in the quatrain with which the play closes:

From hence let those be warned, who mean to wed;
Lest mutual falsehood stain the bridal bed;
For each deceiver to his cost may find,
That marriage-frauds too oft are paid in kind.

The title is an oblique indictment of worldly marriages based on "marriage frauds." At the climax of the play when informed he has "become a cuckold by anticipation," Fainall, formerly so certain he knew "the way of wedlock and the world," fulminates: "... I, it seems, am a husband, a rank husband; and my wife a very arrant, rank wife—all in the way of the world" (*W. W.* III, 3, p. 370). Shortly before the denouement Fainall, aware that if he charges his wife and Mirabell with adultery they may counter with proof of his own adultery with Marwood, cynically accepts the inevitable: "If it must all come out, why let 'em know it; 'tis but the way of the world" (V, 3, p. 407). As the intrigue and counterintrigue unfolds, Fainall's predatory demands for possession of legacies increase; first he covets half of Millamant's fortune, then all of his wife's fortune, and finally all of Lady Wishfort's fortune. Fainall's attempted extortion is unexpectedly checked in the denouement when Mirabell defeats him by producing "the deed of gift in trust":[4]

Fain. ... What's here?—Damnation! [*Reads.*] 'A deed of conveyance of the whole estate real ... in trust to Edward Mirabell.'—Confusion!

Mir. Even so, sir; 'tis the Way of the World, sir, of the widows of the world. (V, 3, p. 409)

The plot is primarily a struggle between two pairs of adulterers for the control of three legacies;[5] the initial intrigue based on the Sir Rowland hoax; the counterintrigue on an exposure of the identity of Sir Rowland, a threatened divorce to avenge adultery, and a series of extortions to requite cuckoldry. The plot does not gyrate continually about Mirabell and Millamant;[6] instead it evolves out of the hopes and fears of the four adulterers as they scheme to snare the ambivalent Lady Wishfort into an irrevocable disposal of the legacies. Unless this group of five is regarded as the center of the action, the entire play lacks unity; and neither the zany courtships nor the proviso scene of the fourth act are integrated with the aftermath of adultery theme. Moreover, the increased tempo and heightened suspense of the fifth act—emanating from Fainall's attempted extortion, his wife's denial of the unchastity charge, and Lady Wishfort's bewildered ambivalence—seem forced and melodramatic; and above all, the surprise rising from producing the valid deed of conveyance will seem merely a meretricious excrescence instead of an "artful solution of the *fable.*"

The *carpe diem* philosophy which permeates the "May-January triangles" of the subplots of Etherege's comedies and those of Congreve's three earlier plays never penetrates deeply in *The Way of the World*. Glib rake and wanton wife no longer plunge into adultery with exuberant zest. Nor does an insolent assurance and a series of plausible evasions mislead the wronged cuckold. Adultery, attempted or consummated, is no longer quibbled out of existence. Rake and wanton are held responsible, indeed accountable for past and present transgressions. The rake, witty and willful though he may be, is unable to evade the consequences of his own or his partner's licentiousness. In *The Way of the World* life is regarded not as a pageant but as a sequence of integrated experiences in which the present is invariably conditioned by the past and foreshadows the future.

The inhabitants of the world depicted in this comedy are not citizens, nor nobility, but gentry. They are no longer ramping toward gentility as they do in many earlier comedies; they have arrived. Their milieu is no longer the fringes of the court, nor the stall, nor the counting house of the citizen. They are established in the drawing room from which they occasionally saunter into the park, or to the chocolate house. The "way" of each is willful, often egoistic; the end of each is security and leisure; the pride of each is sophistication; and wit is frequently used to refine upon pleasure and to evaluate taste, manners, and morals. This brittle world of leisure and sophistication, like the Roman world upon which it is modeled, is rooted in inherited wealth. To remain in this coterie, wealth is essential; and throughout this comedy all the intrigue and counterintrigue of the adulterers center on retaining or obtaining legacies. Congreve's protest against the way of the world is that of a man of reflective judgment who sees that happiness and the dignity of life are sacrificed to an exaggerated care for the means of living, to predatory legacy seeking, to false values, to the slavery of some ruling passion or appetite, to intellectual brilliance tarnished by moral weakness.

Congreve is not an apologist for, but rather a satirist of the way of the world. He castigates vice on two moral levels by contrasting the punishment of a pair of transgressors on the way to reformation with that of a pair on the way to degradation. Since the rake, the adulteress, the cast mistress, and the cuckold are astute, they are aware of their own social and emotional predicaments; consequently the play and interplay of their emotions and motives take on a deeper and subtler ethical significance. Unlike those buoyant comedies based on the initial stages of illicit intrigue, *The Way of the World* reveals the deceit and dissension rife in the final stages of adulterous intimacy; consequently the spirit of these scenes is not that of avid expectation but rather that of sated disillusionment. The effect of adultery on the integration or disintegration of character is stressed; the transgressors by their conscious response to situations engendered by vicious conduct are ultimately either restored to integrity or branded with infamy.)

The major plot complications emanating from the legacy conflict center on Lady Wishfort and the four transgressors. Mirabell and Mrs. Fainall, once guilty of an illicit union, have broken off their affair before the play begins; Fainall and Mrs. Marwood, guilty of an adulterous intimacy, remain professed lovers (at least to each other) throughout the play. A constant fear of exposure of "marriage frauds" breeds suspicion and distrust, since each of the four is astute enough to realize that if his adultery were exposed to the puritanical Lady Wishfort all he most values would become increasingly unattainable. "Hampered" by former indiscretions, the transgressors scheme to maintain coterie prestige, to achieve emotional stability, and above all, to assure financial security. The coterie prestige of the four depends upon an ability to conceal former adultery. The emotional stability rests on a number of factors—for Mirabell, to wed Millamant; for Marwood, to snare Mirabell either as lover or as husband; for Fainall, to possess wealth sufficient to indulge profligacy; and for Mrs. Fainall, either to separate from or gain ascendancy over her licentious mate. The financial security depends upon the disposal of the legacies of Millamant, Mrs. Fainall, and Lady Wishfort.

A close analysis of five hitherto neglected scenes will show how Congreve in the spirit of Horace and Jonson satirizes avarice and adultery. Throughout *The Way of the World* every character who has indulged in illicit relations finds that his present or past adultery hampers his ability to plan for the future—that immorality cannot be quibbled out of existence.

In Act I, Scene 1, Mirabell and Fainall fence with evasions to reach inferences. Both are eager to discover why Marwood has thwarted a clandestine marriage between the heiress Millamant, and the reformed rake, Mirabell. Each suspects that the other is the lover of Marwood and therefore knows more about her motives for blocking the marriage than he cares or dares to admit. To conceal his perplexity, Fainall affects an air of cynical detachment and makes licentious generalizations which appear to be an end in themselves. (Mingled with the fencing between Fainall and Mirabell are fragments of retrospective dialogue, an understanding of which is essential for a knowledge of motives which activate the intrigue and counterintrigue, but the significance of this dialogue is overshadowed by the brilliance of the wit.) Mirabell, sensing his adversary's intent is to conceal not to reveal his relation to Marwood and his role in the legacy intrigue, resorts to the same sort of epigrammatic innuendo that Fainall is using:

Mir. ... But for the discovery of this amour I am indebted to your friend, or your wife's friend, Mrs. Marwood.

Fain. What should provoke her to be your enemy, unless she has made you advances which you have slighted? Women do not easily forgive omissions of that nature.

Mir. She was always civil to me till of late.—I confess I am not one of those coxcombs who are apt to ... think that she who does not refuse 'em everything, can refuse 'em nothing.

Fain. You are a gallant man, Mirabell; and though you may

have cruelty enough not to satisfy a lady's longing, you have too much generosity not to be tender of her honour. Yet you speak with an indifference which seems to be affected, and confesses you are conscious of a negligence.

Mir. You pursue the argument with a distrust that seems to be unaffected, and confesses you are conscious of a concern for which the lady is more indebted to you than is your wife. (pp. 321–322)

In the fencing between Mirabell and Fainall just quoted as well as in that between Marwood and Mrs. Fainall, to follow, a satirical irony emerges because, all dissembling notwithstanding, neither character, however astute, is able to discover his adversary's secret without first disclosing his own. Each verbal snooper encounters a shock like that of a keyhole peeper who peering in sees an eye staring out. Just as Fainall, in his eagerness to determine whether Marwood has made amorous advances to Mirabell, betrays undue concern about a woman who isn't his wife, so Mrs. Fainall, in her zeal to prove that Marwood loves Mirabell, betrays an indiscreet interest in a man who isn't her husband.

Act II opens with the castoff mistress of Mirabell and the sated mistress of Fainall exchanging cynical observations on love and lovers. However, the cynicism of their remarks is not a gratuitous display of wit; it is a pretense of candor to beget confidence; a bait to trap a confession of adherence to libertinism. Scenting the trap, Mrs. Fainall does not confess herself a libertine, instead she professes to be a staunch adherent of the conventions elaborated in Lady Wishfort's cabal sessions—an antagonism toward men and an aversion to marriage. From man, the fencing veers to a man, Mirabell, since each hopes to fathom her antagonist's feeling for and past and present relation to him. The dialogue continues with protestations of plain dealing followed by hypocritical cant and deliberately misleading candor. Finally, Marwood admits an inclination to become the wife of Mirabell but claims as sole motive the desire to rack him with fear and jealousy. Such distortion of truth irks Mrs. Fainall, who, forgetting to conceal her own feelings for the rake, accuses Mrs. Marwood of dissembling hatred and then defends Mirabell's virtues with a warmth which inadvertently discloses her own partiality for him:

Mrs. Fain. Ay, Ay, dear Marwood, if we will be happy, we must find the means in ourselves, and among ourselves. Men are ever in extremes; either doating or averse. While they are lovers, if they have fire and sense, their jealousies are insupportable; and when they cease to love ... they loath ...

Mrs. Mar. True, 'tis an unhappy circumstance of life ... that the man so often should outlive the lover. (II, 1, p. 335)

.   .   .   .

Mrs. Fain. Ingenious mischief! would thou wert married to Mirabell.

Mrs. Mar. Would I were!

Mrs. Fain. You change colour.

Mrs. Mar. Because I hate him.

Mrs. Fain. So do I; but I can hear him named. But what reason have you to hate him in particular?

Mrs. Mar. I never loved him; he is, and always was, insufferably proud.

Mrs. Fain. By the reason you give for your aversion, one would think it dissembled; for you have laid a fault to his charge, of which his enemies must acquit him.

Mrs. Mar. Oh then, it seems, you are one of his favourable enemies! Methinks you look a little pale, and now you flush again. (p. 337)

The mercurial wit which seeks evasions to conceal "unseasonable truths" is at once Congreve's bane and glory: it is his bane because it exacts too rapid, too penetrating, too sustained powers of discernment from audience or reader; it is his glory because it reveals hidden springs of action which lead to subtle characterization and motivation. Closely akin to the mercurial wit of the two probing scenes is the astringent wit of the three altercation scenes, in which a pair of adulterers fence with irony, sarcasm, and innuendo to reach inferences about the marriage and adultery frauds.

Near the end of Scene 1, Act II, a crisis in the affairs of Fainall and Mrs. Marwood is presented: "Two artful people, who, from satiety, are heartily tired of each other, and only from convenience and mutual interest keep up a correspondence, accidentally quarrel; and, from a collision of their passions, they not only unfold their own actions and characters, but open the preceding transactions necessary to be known by the audience. ... It is indeed a happy imitation of Ben Jonson's manner of ... explanation of characters by sudden altercation."[7]

When Mrs. Fainall sweeps off the stage accompanied by Mirabell, Mrs. Marwood, regretful of having confided her marital ambitions to a rival enamoured of Mirabell, suggests that she and Fainall follow them. Fainall accuses his mistress of undue interest in Mirabell; she parries he has cause to watch his wife. But the charge that Marwood levels against Mrs. Fainall, the husband twists against his mistress. Hearing his wife's fidelity questioned, Fainall does not insist upon her innocence; instead he shrewdly points out his mistress' guilt:

Fain. You would intimate, then, as if there were a fellow-feeling between my wife and him.

Mrs. Mar. I think she does not hate him to that degree she would be thought.

Fain. But he, I fear, is too insensible.

Mrs. Mar. It may be you are deceived.

Fain. It may be so. I do now begin to apprehend it.

Mrs. Mar. What?

Fain. That I have been deceived, madam, and you are false.

Mrs. Mar. That I am false! What mean you?

Fain. To let you know I see through all your little arts.—Come, you both love him; and both have equally dissembled your aversion. (pp. 338–339)

Mrs. Marwood alleges she hates Mirabell, challenges her accuser to prove her false; he taunts her with former hypocrisies and she, stung to the quick, threatens to expose Fainall's avarice and adultery:

Mrs. Mar. ... I challenge you to show an instance that can confirm your groundless accusation. I hate him.

Fain. And wherefore do you hate him? he is insensible, and your resentment follows his neglect. An instance! the injuries you have done him are a proof: your interposing in his love. What cause had you to make discoveries of his pretended passion? to undeceive the credulous aunt, and be the officious obstacle of his match with Millamant?

Mrs. Mar. My obligations to my lady urged me; I had professed a friendship to her; and could not see her easy nature so abused by that dissembler.

Fain. What, was it conscience then? Professed a friendship! O the pious friendships of the female sex!

Mrs. Mar. More tender, more sincere, and more enduring, than all the vain and empty vows of men, whether professing love to us, or mutual faith to one another.

Fain. Ha! ha! ha! you are my wife's friend too.

Mrs. Mar. Shame and ingratitude! do you reproach me? you, you upbraid me? Have I been false to her, through strict fidelity to you, and sacrificed my friendship to keep my love inviolate?...

Fain. You misinterpret my reproof. I meant but to remind you of the slight account you once could make of strictest ties, when set in competition with your love to me.

Mrs. Mar. 'Tis false, you urged it with deliberate malice! 'twas spoken in scorn, and I never will forgive it.

Fain. Your guilt, not your resentment, begets your rage. If yet you loved, you could forgive a jealousy: but you are stung to find you are discovered.

Mrs. Mar. It shall be all discovered. ... I'll publish to the world the injuries you have done me, both in my fame and fortune! With both I trusted you, you bankrupt in honour, as indigent of wealth. (pp. 339–340)

Partly because she is aware of her lover's mercenary duplicity, and partly because she wants to sever old ties before she pursues Mirabell, Mrs. Marwood seizes this occasion to cast Fainall aside, but he does not choose to let her leave while threats to expose his vice and greed still burn on her lips. Finally aware that Mrs. Marwood craves a husband, not a lover, Fainall proposes divorcing his wife and marrying his mistress. As the emotional tension increases, the scene ends in uncontrolled disgust on one side, impassioned pleading on the other:

Fain. You know I love you.

Mrs. Mar. Poor dissembling! ... well, it is not yet— ... too late;—I have that comfort.

Fain. It is, [too late] to love another.

Mrs. Mar. But not to loathe, detest, abhor mankind, myself, and the whole treacherous world.

Fain. Nay, this is extravagance.—Come, I ask your pardon—no tears—I was to blame, I could not love you and be easy in my doubts. Pray forbear—I believe you; I'm convinced I've done you wrong; and any way, every way will make amends. I'll hate my wife yet more, damn her! I'll part with her, rob her of all she's worth, and we'll retire somewhere. ... I'll marry thee—be pacified. (pp. 341–342)

In the preceding scene a libertine and a wanton have stolen away together, but instead of an exhibition of erotic dalliance in the *carpe diem* vein, we are shown the grim spectacle of the consequences of adultery. The source of comedy is not lodged in the physical manifestations of illicit passion but in the emotional tension engendered by it. The adulteress' futile attempts to extricate herself from a tedious sensual entanglement; the adulterer's resentment rising from the discovery of his sated mistress' desire to pursue another gallant; the clouds of evasion, hypocrisy, and duplicity finally torn asunder by bolts of recrimination—a Jonsonian scene of vice clawing vice.

In Act II, Scene 2, as in the foregoing scene, an exposition of "marriage frauds" which took place before the play opens permits the cast mistress to subject her lover to a tirade; just as Mrs. Marwood berates Fainall for having robbed her of "fame and fortune," so does Mrs. Fainall chide Mirabell for having deprived her of "love and liberty." In one breath Mrs. Fainall reviles her absent husband; in the next, reminds her former lover of past "favors," and blames him for having urged her incompatible marriage. To check his cast mistress' complaints and reminiscences, Mirabell first indulges in "refined cynicism," then finally turns the conversation from illicit relations in the past to licit relations in the future:

Mrs. Fain. While I only hated my husband, I could bear to see him; but since I have despised him, he's too offensive.

Mir. O you should hate with prudence.

Mrs. Fain. Yes, for I have loved with indiscretion.

Mir. You should have just so much disgust for your husband, as may be sufficient to make you relish your lover.

Mrs. Fain. You have been the cause that I have loved without bounds, and would you set limits to that aversion of which you have been the occasion? Why did you make me marry this man? (pp. 342–343)

Mirabell reminds Mrs. Fainall why a woman of wealth was advised to marry a pauper, calculating thereby to convert her reproachful retrospections into recollection of indebtedness:

Mir. Why do we daily commit disagreeable and dangerous actions? to save that idol, reputation. If the familiarities of our loves had produced that consequence of which you were apprehensive, where could you have fixed a father's name with credit, but on a husband? I knew Fainall to be a man lavish of his morals … yet one whose wit and outward fair behaviour have gained a reputation with the town enough to make that woman stand excused who has suffered herself to be won by his addresses. A better man ought not to have been sacrificed to the occasion; a worse had not answered to the purpose.[8] (p. 343)

By recalling that when his mistress was about to show the effects of having loved with indiscretion, her lover contrived a worldly marriage to shield her from slander, Mirabell indicates that although he has no intention of resuming illicit relations, he did and still does desire to preserve her reputation. Since her querulous reference to their past intimacy reveals that she is still too fond of her erstwhile lover to deny him anything, he urges that she intercede to preserve his (marriage) "contract" with Millamant. Confident that Mrs. Fainall will sacrifice her pride to prove her loyalty, Mirabell gives her a detailed description of the Sir Rowland hoax, and by making her privy to his design, empowers her to ruin or to advance his fortune.

After Marwood is inadvertently informed of the Sir Rowland hoax, each pair of schemers contends against tangible intrigue instead of fencing with innuendo to reach inferences; consequently from this point on the dialogue grows less cryptic and the conflict grows more open and bitter (III, 1, pp. 357–358). So nearly equal are protagonists with antagonists in tenacity and ingenuity that imminent victory shifts from side to side through a sequence of well-motivated reversals.

In Act III, Scene 3, Mrs. Marwood is aware that mutual interests make it advisable for her to forget past grievances and again insinuate herself into Fainall's good graces. Three important disclosures which she overheard when hidden in Lady Wishfort's closet (III, 2, pp. 357–359) have changed her attitude toward Fainall: the first, that Mirabell "can't abide her," transforms love to hate; the other two, that Mrs. Fainall is Mirabell's former mistress and that Sir Rowland is Mirabell's disguised servant, arm her to punish the rake immune to her charm. In order to carry out her scheme for vengeance against the reformed rake, Mrs. Marwood seeks the aid of the dishonored husband, arousing Fainall's resentment by informing him of his wife's adultery with Mirabell.

Fainall can affect and sustain an attitude of detachment only so long as he himself is not emotionally involved. When Fainall hears of his wife's infidelity his cynical detachment is shattered. His pride in having outwitted his detested wife by having carried on a clandestine affair under her very nose had buoyed him up to endure matrimony. Besides, his was a marriage of convenience. His ego smarts when he discovers that his wife's motive for accepting him as a husband was no less worldly than his in tolerating her as a wife. He coveted her money to indulge his profligacy; she needed his name to preserve her reputation. Avarice had blinded Fainall; he failed to suspect that the wealthy widow he married was the former mistress of Mirabell:

Fain. ... I, it seems, am a husband, a rank husband; and my wife a very arrant, rank wife—all in the way of the world. 'Sdeath, to be a cuckold by anticipation, a cuckold in embryo! sure I was born with budding antlers, like a young satyr. ... 'Sdeath! to be out-witted—to be out-jilted—out-matrimony'd!—If I had kept my speed like a stag, 'twere somewhat,—but to crawl after, with my horns, like a snail, and be outstripped by my wife—'tis scurvy wedlock. (p. 370)

Fainall, for the moment, is too nettled to think, so Mrs. Marwood advises him to bridle his rage, suggests there is always the possibility of a separation, and points out the profitable thing to do is to undermine Mirabell's Sir Rowland hoax. Mrs. Marwood then proposes a counterintrigue which will enable Fainall to extort the portion of his wife's wealth to which he does not yet hold title as well as the entire fortune of Millamant. She points out that if the abused husband act wary and wrathful his horns "may prove a cap of maintenance." Her strategem is based partly on her knowledge of Fainall's mercenary nature, and partly on her familiarity with Lady Wishfort's love for Mrs. Fainall and fear of scandal:

Mrs. Mar. You married her to keep you; and if you can contrive to have her keep you better than you expected, why should you not keep her longer than you intended.

Fain. The means, the means.

Mrs. Mar. Discover to my lady your wife's conduct; threaten to part with her!—my lady loves her, and will come to any composition to save her reputation. Take the opportunity of breaking it, just upon the discovery of this imposture [Sir Rowland hoax]. My lady will be enraged beyond bounds, and sacrifice niece, and fortune, and all, at that conjuncture. (pp. 370–371)

After Mrs. Marwood suggests a way to avenge cuckoldry by extorting legacies, Fainall rationalizes cuckoldry into an honorable state. Superficially regarded, his casuistry on his own cuckoldry is refined cynicism devoid of emotion; intrinsically it is an escape from a reality too grim and painful to face. His wit is a fragile web of words over an abyss of disillusionment. His judgment is paralyzed by his own sophistry:

Fain. ... Let me see—I am married already, so that's over:—my wife has played the jade with me—well, that's over too: —I never loved her, or if I had, why that would have been over too by this time:—jealous of her I cannot be, for I am certain; so there's an end of jealousy:—weary of her I am, and shall be—no, there's no end of that—no, no, that were too much to hope. Thus far concerning my repose; now for my reputation. As to my own, I married not for it, so that's out of the question;—and as to my part in my wife's—why, she had parted with her's before; so bringing none to me, she can take none from me; 'tis against all rule of play, that I should lose to one who has not wherewithal to stake.

Mrs. Mar. Besides, you forget, marriage is honourable.

Fain. Hum, faith, and that's well thought on; marriage is honourable as you say; and if so, wherefore should cuckoldom be a discredit, being derived from so honourable a root? (p. 371)

In the mutually predatory relation between Fainall and Marwood, vice preys on vice, spreading a web of devious wit as a snare. Lust and avarice beget duplicity; Marwood's duplicity hardens into malice, Fainall's duplicity leads to self-delusion. Initially, Fainall distorts truth to mislead others, ultimately he himself becomes a victim of his own casuistry. Steeped in dissimulation, Fainall's judgment warps, truth and error mingle and merge and become one; wounded pride battens on false hope and sham loyalty. By the close of the third act Fainall is stripped of this pretenses; he is exposed as "indigent in wealth," "bankrupt in honor," degraded in intellect—a dupe of the mistress he duped. His progressive degeneration culminates in the fifth act, where, throwing off all affectations of breeding, civility, and decency, he emerges as an outright knave—predatory, ruthless, and violent—a variant of the knaves satirized by Jonson, Middleton, and Massinger.

Not one of these five scenes in which the aftermath of adultery is stressed has heretofore been analyzed in detail by any critic in the entire history of Congreve criticism. Most critics have assumed and still assume that the character types, the rake, the cast mistress, the adulteress, and the cuckold portrayed in the foregoing scenes differ little if at all from those in the comedies of Congreve's predecessors and contemporaries.

Actually these characters did appear with varying modifications in the successfull comedies on the Restoration stage, but the types were almost invariably depicted as embodiments of folly, behaving with abandoned disregard for social taboos, getting into the same inevitable difficulties, extricating themselves with glib evasions, emerging from their escapades little the worse for temporary distress, and expressing their licentious creed in similitude, innuendo, and epigram.

But in *The Way of the World* the four types undergo significant transformations. In Congreve's first three plays, as in those of other dramatists of his day, these four types, all exponents of *carpe diem* philosophy, are indulgently regarded as embodiments of folly and are ridiculed with varying degrees of amused tolerance, whereas in *The Way of the World* the traditional types are modified to emphasize the vicious aspect of licentiousness, and both folly and vice are satirized with an astringent irony. In Congreve's last comedy each transgressor is sufficiently sophisticated to know that scandal and derision follow the exposure of adultery; wayward enough to flout morality even though corrigible enough to reform; consequently, each libertine in turn is either threatened with or subjected to an exposure and a ridicule commensurate with his guilt.

The rake in Congreve's earlier plays—Bellmour in *The Old Bachelor* (*O.B.*); Careless in *The Double-Dealer* (*D.D.*); Scandal in *Love for Love* (*L.L.*)—philanders with a wanton wife, frequently is discovered in compromising situations by the wronged husband, yet with plausible invention wheedles the cuckold into disbelieving his own eyes; thus the transgressor evades the consequence of his entanglement; furthermore Fortune, being but another strumpet, favors the impudent rake, and his final triumph is either to marry a wealthy virgin (*O.B.*), or to remain an irresistible bachelor (*D. D., L. L.*). But in *The Way of the World*, Mirabell, sated with adultery, does no philandering in the play, Fortune jilts the constant lover, Nemesis pursues him, and not until he has suffered for his reputation as a rake, as well as for his former transgressions, is he permitted to marry a wealthy virgin.

The cast mistress (Silvia, *O.B.*; Mrs. Frail, *L.L.*) piqued at being deserted by the man (*O.B.*; men, *L.L.*) to whom she could refuse nothing is disillusioned with love, but wants to marry to mend her reputation. Though she schemes to snare a wit for a husband, she succeeds at best in trapping a witwoud into a masked marriage; her attempt to maintain an unblemished reputation is frustrated by her betrayer (Silvia, Bellmour), and her experiences are chronicled with levity. Unlike the former cast mistress who weds a mental cripple, Mrs. Fainall marries a moral cripple. Mrs. Fainall, although grateful for having her reputation preserved by the rake who seduced her, is cynical about both husbands and lovers. She regrets having had to sacrifice love and freedom to forestall slander; she chafes under the marital yoke, she is forced to bear the indignity of helping her former lover become the husband of another woman, and finally she comes close to being publicly branded an adulteress.

The adulteress (Mrs. Fondlewife, *O.B.*; Mrs. Foresight, *L.L.*; Lady Plyant, *D.D.*), contemptuous of her mate, easy to any gallant, has just sufficient disgust for her husband to make her relish her lover; she has developed a dissembled virtue and an impudent assurance which extricate her from trying situations when her spouse doubts her fidelity; her abandoned liaison with a rake is depicted with gay indulgence. Mrs. Marwood, sated with her married lover, desires Mirabell either as a husband or as a lover. She has perfected a feigned innocence and an egocentric duplicity which serve admirably until her exposure in the denouement, when her malicious intrigues and immorality are unveiled and she is rejected by her coterie.

The cuckold (Fondlewife, *O.B.*; Foresight, *L.L.*; Sir Paul Plyant, *D.D.*), a superannuated eccentric wed to a tempting sybarite, vacillates between ludicrous doubt and absurd faith; he is as often jealous without a cause as satisfied without a reason; his cuckoldom and his reaction to horns are portrayed with derisive ribaldry. Mr. Fainall, a match for his wife in age and sophistication; appraises his associates, indulges their follies, and exploits their vices; preoccupied as he is with cajoling his mistress and scheming to extort legacies, he is unconcerned by his wife's attention to a rake until his discovery that he has been made a "cuckold by anticipation"; his casuistry on cuckoldry fails to minimize his dishonor; and after he goes "horn mad" his progressive degeneration and sheer villainy increase until finally he is faced with the choice of poverty or becoming his wife's dependent.)

Congreve's modifications of the four character types sharpen the satirical implications of their behavior and conversation. As we have interpreted them, the adultery episodes both imply and express a standard of conduct, and violators of morality are subjected to the exposure and derision demanded by Aristotle's theory of comedy which Congreve epitomizes as "... an Imitation of the worse sort of People. ... not ... the worse sort of People in respect to their Quality, but in respect to their Manners [conduct in its moral aspect]. ... the Vices most frequent, and which are the common Practice of the looser sort of Livers, are the subject Matter of Comedy. ... For men are to be laugh'd out of their Vices in Comedy; the Business of Comedy is to delight, as well as to instruct; And as vicious People are made asham'd of their Follies or Faults, by seeing them expos'd in a ridiculous manner, so are good People at once both warn'd and diverted at their Expence." [9]

The repartee of the witty lovers, no less than that of the adulterers, gains in ethical significance and satiric implication when examined in relation to plot, theme, and character. If, instead of being read as an isolated passage, the proviso scene is regarded as the culmination of a sequence of brief encounters between a pair of estranged lovers, their inimitable repartee will be reappraised as something more than frothy banter. Implicit, or explicit—in a few sentences or in an entire episode, interwoven through the first three acts, Congreve has developed a cluster of impediments which obstruct the union of the witty couple. In the interim between the thwarted elopement and the proviso scene, Mirabell and Millamant experience misgivings about the desirability of becoming husband and wife; she is determined not to "dwindle" into a wife, and he is equally resolved not to be "enlarged" into a husband. She is irritated by his gravity and sententiousness, offended by his seeming past and present entanglement with Marwood and Mrs. Fainall. He is tantalized by her caprice, vanity, and coquetry; disturbed by her attraction for and defense of the witwouds. Even when they are alone together pique and suspicion separate them. At the beginning of the proviso scene, the lovers are mutually distrustful of each other's words, acts, and motives. Until due attention is paid to the origin and growth of the estrangement between the witty couple, the serio-comic aspects of this scene will fail to be adequately appreciated.

Wit in the proviso scene is more than brilliant persiflage;[10] it is a means to an end; its purpose is to expose and ridicule the actual follies and incipient vices which if not restrained by taste and judgment lead to "marriage frauds." A man who has been a rake and a woman who still is a coquette contemplate marriage with trepidation. They, having observed the absurd and tragic misunderstandings and duplicities of married friends and acquaintances, attempt to safeguard their anticipated union. Not until the more disastrous shoals have been discovered is this couple ready to venture into matrimony. The provisos, based on a critical observation of the trials and errors of contemporary husbands and wives, are a way to avoid marital friction. Mirabell has experienced adultery and its aftermath, Millamant has merely observed it; consequently his provisos are sounder and more searching than hers. Her major concern is to assure untrammled preservation of liberty; his foremost concern is to forestall unhampered liberty from diverging into license. By supplanting impulse and illusion with reason and truth, Mirabell succeeds not only in dissipating his own fear of phantom horns, but also in pointing a way through compromise to an amicable mean between repression and license.

Millamant states the terms on which she will "dwindle into a wife." All her conditions are designed to avoid the attitudes and behavior which make contemporary marriage insufferable to a high-spirited individual. Insisting she will not have a grossly demonstrative husband she prohibits terms of endearment and all other modes of publicly flaunting either domestic felicity or friction:

Mrs. Mil. ... I won't be called names after I'm married; positively I won't be called names.

Mir. Names!

Mrs. Mil. Ay, as wife, spouse, my dear, joy, jewel, love, sweetheart, and the rest of that nauseous cant, in which men and their wives are so fulsomely familiar—I shall never bear that—good Mirabell, don't let us be familiar or fond, nor kiss before folks, like my Lady Fadler and Sir Francis: nor go to Hyde-park together the first Sunday in a new chariot, to provoke eyes and whispers, and then never to be seen there together again; as if we were proud of one another the first week, and ashamed of one another ever after. ... but let us be very strange and well-bred: let us be as strange as if we had been married a great while; and as well bred as if we were not married at all. (p. 379)

Aware that familiarity breeds contempt, and contempt disparagement, she provides for the preservation of her uncensured personal liberty. Prompted by caution more far-sighted than astute, she demands liberty to associate and communicate with friends who interest her, license to wear clothes which appeal to her, the privilege of being alone when she is out of humor, and the right to a specified degree of privacy at all times:

Mrs. Mil. .... As liberty to pay and receive visits to and from whom I please; to write and receive letters, without interrogatories or wry faces on your part; to wear what I please; and choose conversation with regard only to my own taste; to have no obligation upon me to converse with wits that I don't like, because they are your acquaintance: or to be intimate with fools, because they may be your relations. Come to dinner when I please; dine in my dressing-room when I'm out of humour, without giving a reason. To have my closet inviolate; to be sole empress of my tea-table, which you must never presume to approach without first asking leave. And lastly, wherever I am, you shall always knock at the door before you come in. (p. 379)

All Millamant's provisos are the result of her desire to prolong and increase the prenuptial glamour. Unquestionably, her charm, consciously cultivated though it be, emanates from something more enduring than scent, more tangible than similitudes. Cognizant as she is that much of her personal witchery results from delicately nurtured airs, artifices, and affectations which are best fostered by freedom and privacy, she bans the despotism and prying curiosity which lead to disillusionment.

The terms upon which Mirabell agrees to become "a tractable and complying husband" display marked vision and discernment. Because he sees possible disaster lurking in some of Millamant's provisos, he limits and qualifies her demands. In a society where malice and slander run rampant, appearance must be taken into account; honor depends on seeming as well as being chaste. He begins by conditioning her license to choose friends and her liberty to come and go by insisting that he first be reassured that her conduct will never be such as would destroy respect and confidence—that her liberty never deviate into license:

Mir. ... —Well, have I liberty to offer conditions—that when you are dwindled into a wife, I may not be beyond measure enlarged into a husband?

. . . .

Mir. .... I covenant, that your acquaintance be general; that you admit no sworn confidant, or intimate of your own sex; no she friend to screen her affairs under your countenance, and tempt you to make trial of a mutual secrecy. No decoy duck to wheedle you a fop-scrambling to the play in a mask—then bring you home in a pretended fright, when you think you shall be found out— and rail at me for missing the play, and disappointing the frolic which you had to pick me up, and prove my constancy. ... I shut my doors against all bawds with baskets, and pennyworths of muslin, china, fans .... (p. 380)

Mirabell grants Millamant freedom to determine her own mode of personal adornment providing, in her zeal to improve her face or figure, she never be led astray by fashionable excesses. He bans cosmetics and strait lacing; because he values natural beauty above artificial pulchritude and a hardy heir above a shapely wife. His experience in coping with the conflicting ways of the world has sharpened his ability to separate values that are permanent from those that are transitory, values that are fundamental from those that are superficial:

Mir. I article, that you continue to like your own face, as long as I shall: and while it passes current with me, that you endeavour not to new-coin it. To which end, together with all vizards for the day, I prohibit all masks for the night, made of oiled-skins, and I know not what—hogs' bones, hares' gall, pig-water, and the marrow of a roasted cat ... when you shall be breeding ... Which may be presumed with a blessing on our endeavours. ... I denounce against all strait lacing, squeezing for a shape, till you mould my boy's head like a sugar-loaf, and instead of a man child, make me father to a crooked billet. (p. 380)

If Millamant will agree not to cultivate the masculine vice of indulgence in strong liquors, Mirabell is willing never to violate the privacy of her tea table. Probably with Lady Wishfort's weakness for ratafia and cherry brandy in mind, he distinguishes sharply between tea-table and tavern beverages.

Mir. ... Lastly, to the dominion of the tea-table I submit—but with proviso, that you exceed not in your province; but restrain yourself to native and simple tea-table drinks, as tea, chocolate, and coffee ... I banish all foreign forces, all auxiliaries to the tea-table, as orange-brandy, all aniseed, cinnamon, citron, and Barbadoes waters, together with ratafia, and the most noble spirit of clary—but for cowslip wine, poppy water, and all dormitives, those I allow. (pp. 380–381)

Enough dialogue has been quoted to show that though both lovers alike are witty, they are not witty alike; the wit of Mirabell is predominantly judicial, that of Millamant is fanciful. Not until after fancy tempers his judgment, and judgment curbs her fancy does the fencing end in a truce.

The surface brilliance of the dialogue in this scene, as critics have already pointed out, marks the culmination of Congreve's wit. But there is far more than surface brilliance; here, Congreve combines a surface of sparkling wit with an undercurrent of penetrating insight, and so harmonious is the combination that neither the surface of sallies nor the undercurrent of sense has been sacrificed. The verve with which the provisos are phrased shows that Congreve can be gay without being trivial, as well as serious without being solemn. The reflective overtones of this dialogue could not have been written in a mood of irresponsible detachment nor in a mood of licentious cynicism; ever present beneath the scintillating wit is the conviction that unchecked indulgence in folly often ends in vice; that unrestrained affectation may degenerate into immorality.

When, as Congreve probably intended, Mirabell's way of reflective compromise, as developed in the proviso scene (Act IV), is contrasted with Fainall's way of cynical opportunism, as developed in the climax near the close of the altercation scene in Act III, Mirabell's progressive regeneration is as apparent as Fainall's progressive degeneration. Mirabell's vigilance in the proviso scene to foresee and forestall the degree of liberty which leads to license is anticipated in the altercation scene where he checks his mistress' attempt to resume an adulterous relationship. In sharp contrast to Mirabell's growing sense of responsibility is Fainall's increased irresponsibility; at the end of Act III, as well as throughout Act V, Fainall and his mistress plunge deeper in licentiousness, extortion, and violence.

On the surface, the conflict between the adulterers in Act V is intensely emotional and grimly realistic; beneath the surface, heightening the regeneration-degeneration motif and the suspense of the ebb and flow of the action, is a vein of unobtrusive dramatic irony. This dramatic irony plays variations on the theme of the duper duped, as it runs through the series of surprises and reversals. It is a pervasive irony—incisive, caustic, and astringent. Congreve's irony raises this play, and especially its fifth act, from the level of melodrama to the summit of satiric comedy.

To appreciate the technical perfection of the complex fifth act, to understand how the ingenious suspense is sustained by foreshadowing, reversal, discovery, and surprise, and above all, to note how the subtle irony underlying the suspense sharpens the contrast between reputation and character, and between appearance and reality, it is necessary to subject this act to a close analysis.

To trace the fusion of legacy conflict with dramatic irony we discuss in turn, three crises, the denouement, and the conclusion; the first crisis, (Scene 1) foreshadows the victory of the protagonists. The second crisis is an altercation scene centering on an exposure of "marriage frauds." The audience and Mrs. Fainall are aware, but Marwood and Lady Wishfort are unaware, that the position of the antagonists is weakened; that of the protagonists strengthened by a number of discoveries related in the first crisis (Scene 1): Lady Wishfort has been prevented from reading the adultery charges against the protagonists made in the "anonymous" letter written by Marwood. Two servants have caught the antagonists in adultery but have been coerced into swearing an oath of secrecy; they have discovered their oath is no longer binding because it was sworn on a book of poems, not the "Book of Holy Writ"; and consequently these two eyewitnesses are ready and eager to testify where and when the antagonists were caught in *flagrante delicto*. Ironically enough, Foible, the very person who inadvertently disclosed the protagonists' adultery to Marwood (III, 1), deliberately exposes the antagonists' adultery to Mrs. Fainall.

Scene 2 opens with an intimate chat in which Marwood insidiously urges the advisability of Lady Wishfort's compounding with Fainall for the frailties of her daughter. Marwood's guile is not suspected since the guardian, characteristically obtuse, acknowledges, as benefits conferred, a series of injuries Marwood has inflicted upon her daughter, her niece, and herself. However, as soon as the daughter enters, the chat is turned into a conflict. The two adulteresses exchange volleys of charges and countercharges into the ears of the befuddled mother. Because Lady Wishfort is professedly puritanical Mrs. Marwood must conceal her intimacy with Fainall if she hopes to exploit the licentiousness of his wife; the wife must prove Marwood's adultery with Fainall to discredit the censure of his mistress. In response to her opponent's charge of adultery, Mrs. Fainall must deny her own guilt and prove the guilt of her accuser. Confronted on one side with the duplicity of her "friend," on the other with the assurance of her daughter, the gullible Lady cannot decide whom to believe, whom to trust.

After repeatedly defying her opponent by denying the adultery charge, Mrs. Fainall leaves her mother alone with her false friend. Marwood then convinces the Lady that she must accede to Fainall's extortionate demand to spare herself and her daughter from the scandal which a public divorce would unleash. The foundress of the cabal that came together "like the coroner's inquest, to sit upon the murdered reputations of the week" (I, 1, p. 321) is made to feel what it means to be a victim of scandal. The Lady who reduced scandal to a drawing-room diversion is frightened at the prospect of becoming the victim of her own vice:

Mrs. Mar. Prove it, madam! What, and have your name prostituted in a public court! yours and your daughter's reputation worried at the bar by a pack of bawling lawyers! To be ushered in with an O yes of scandal; and have your case opened by an old fumbling lecher in a quoif like a man-midwife; to bring your daughter's infamy to light; to be a theme for legal punsters and quibblers by the statute; and become a jest against a rule of court, where there is no precedent for a jest in any record—not even in doomsday-book; to discompose the gravity of the bench, and provoke naughty interrogatories in more naughty law Latin; while the good judge, tickled with the proceeding, simpers under a grey beard, and fidgets off and on his cushion as if the had swallowed cantharides, or sat upon cow-itch! (V, 2, p. 399)

Throughout the second crisis, Marwood is at the height of her dissimulation but she is unaware that her position has already been undermined. She, the very person who threatens her friend with scandal, is herself to become the prey of scandal. While the mistress arrogantly presses the adultery charge against the wife, she fails to wonder why the wife so confidently denies it; Marwood is unaware that the servants have already revealed her own adultery to the wife she has been accusing of adultery. Nemesis is at Marwood's heels, but she fails to hear a footfall. Scandal becomes a boomerang. The hypocrite who directs it at the reputation of others finds it recoils upon her own.

In crisis three, irony merges with satire on the stupidity and selfishness of the irresponsible guardian. Lady Wishfort is more irked by Fainall's condition that she agree never to marry than she is pleased by his permission to retain her own legacy or perturbed by his demand that she sign away control of the legacies belonging to her niece and daughter. After Fainall leaves, the niece's fortune appears to be safe from his grasp when Millamant professes herself willing to marry Sir Wilfull. After Mirabell enters and assures the guardian that he can and will protect her daughter's legacy, the volatile lady readily forgets her former fears and reverts to coquetry.

Restoration comedy abounds with guardians who are humor characters, but Lady Wishfort overshadows them all. Her humor is lechery like that of the collegiates in *Epicoene*, and the Ladies Tailbush and Eitherside in *The Devil is an Ass*. This superannuated coquette is a complex of contradictions. The guardian who herself needs a guardian, the carnal Puritan who expresses an aversion to men, yet has an "itch to marry," and justifies female frailty with the phrase, "what's integrity to an opportunity" is, at the end of Scene 2, adrift from reality, and, as her name indicates, revels in her own susceptibility to passion: "*Lady Wish*. [*Aside*.] Oh, he has witchcraft in his eyes and tongue!—When I did not see him, I could have bribed a villain to his assassination; but his appearance rakes the embers which have so long lain smothered in my breast" (p. 405).

The deed of conveyance in the denouement has been regarded as a *deus ex machina*, brought in to resolve a complex plot based on courtship intrigue—a plot so intricate, so burdened with surprise and reversal that any aesthetic or ethical purpose the dramatist may have had in mind is totally obscured, if not eclipsed. If, as we have insisted, the plot be regarded as a legacy conflict centered on the four adulterers and Lady Wishfort, not as a plot of courtship centered on Mirabell and Millamant, then, and only then, will the aesthetic and ethical implications of the action emerge with unequivocal clarity. There are not one but two deeds of conveyance involved; the one that Fainall has extorted from his wife, the other that Mirabell foresaw the need of and provided to protect Fainall's wife from her husband's avarice and chicanery. Actually, the only complete surprise in the entire denouement is that Mirabell, not Fainall, holds the valid deed in trust.

Besides resolving the conflict in the denouement and determining the award of poetic justice in the conclusion, this crowning surprise is the crest of the irony; the document upon which Fainall's extortion depended and upon which his serio-comic hybris battened, is proved invalid; ironically the double-dealer whose life has been a sham meets shattering defeat through overconfidence in a spurious document.

The three "surprises" in the denouement are surprises only to Lady Wishfort, the antagonists, the two witwouds, and an inattentive reader or audience. All three surprises have been foreshadowed: The Millamant-Sir Wilfull match is hinted at in V, 1; the eyewitness account of the antagonists' adultery is developed at length in V, 1; Fainall's possession of a deed of conveyance is discussed in detail at the close of Act III. Each of the three foreshadowed "surprises" leads in succession to a well-motivated reversal; and each reversal in turn develops into a test of Fainall's character. In each test, Fainall chooses to disregard civilized restraints which reason and decency have imposed to safeguard man from his own inhumanity. During the first test, Fainall insolently divests himself of all pretense to gratitude, compassion, or concern for a broken promise; during the second, he cynically strips himself of shame and concern for reputation or scandal; during the third, he violently casts off all bonds of civilization and reverts to barbarism. Fainall's hybris, which seems to surmount a series of reversals, ends in the ignominious destruction of his own humanity. In the tradition of Volpone and Sir Giles Overreach, the biter is bit; Fainall is exposed as a bully, a craven, a knave, and a fool.

In the course of the conflict between the adulterers both Mirabell and Fainall have wronged others, as well as been wronged by others; but Fainall, thinking only of the extent others have wronged him, feels justified in avenging fancied as well as real wrongs; whereas Mirabell, seeing the extent he has wronged others, feels obligated to make such restitution as still lies in his power. Mirabell, not a static but a developing character, sets the moral norm, a norm which, like his character, broadens and deepens as the play unfolds. Aware that his intrigue has called into being the counterintrigue which unleashed the folly and vice of his antagonists, Mirabell attempts to right the deliberate and inadvertent wrongs he has inflicted on others. In the process of making amends he shows stamina enough to win and wed Milla-mant despite the numerous obstacles in his path, humanity enough to protect those who need protection against the baser part of their own as well as the baser part of others' nature, and wisdom enough to insist upon compromise, when, as at the close of the play, compromise through mutual tolerance of human frailty seems the only possible way to salvage the Fainalls' mar-riage. The suggested way to reunion is not the sentimental solution of easy tears and sudden repentance, but a rational, a realistic way—a series of calculated risks, of mutual concessions, of gradual adjustments—requiring time, tact, and forbearance.

The play closes with assurances that both lovers and spouses will be reunited; the device used to facilitate both the union of the witty couple and the anticipated reunion of the Fainalls is the deed in trust. Immediately preceding the quatrain before the final curtain, Lady Wishfort, sobered by her ordeal, displays an un-expected dignity of feeling (if not of diction) in her solicitude for her daughter's welfare. Mirabell sensitively perceives the cause of her uneasiness and dispels her fears by attesting that Fainall must accept his wife's terms:

Lady Wish. As I am a person, I can hold out no longer;—I have wasted my spirits so to-day already, that I am ready to sink under the fatigue; and I cannot but have some fears upon me yet, that my son Fainall will pursue some desperate course.

Mir. Madam, disquiet not yourself on that account; to my knowledge his circumstances are such he must of force comply. For my part, I will contribute all that in me lies to a reunion; in the mean time, madam,—[*To* Mrs. Fainall.] let me before these witnesses restore to you this deed of trust; it may be a means, well-managed, to make you live easily together. (pp. 410–411)

Mirabell's humane use of power is rooted in the assumption that man is potentially corrigible; Fainall's cynical abuse of power stems from his conviction that man is fundamentally corrupt. Both men are astute, both reflect on experience, both judge the acts and motives of others by what they know about themselves. But Fainall finds only evil veneered with affected good in himself, therefore he assumes all men are either knaves or fools; if knaves, they, like him, feign goodness; if fools, they are at best potentially vicious, hence the foreordained prey of the predatory knave. Mirabell recognizes that man's character is mixed, that good and evil lie together at the core of his being, yet he chooses to follow a way of life based on the assumption that love, trust, and responsibility are essential elements in human character and society. Fainall, confident that man is primarily evil and that only the weak and the stupid are good, follows a devious way based on the assumption that lust, deceit, and malice are dominant elements in human character and society. Mirabell's way of reflective compromise leads through candor and trust to self-appraisal, culminating in reorientation to reality and eventual regeneration; whereas Fainall's way of cynical opportunism leads through duplicity and distrust to self-deception and terminates in disorientation and degeneration.

The role of Mirabell, like the plot of the play in which he is protagonist, is singularly shifting and complex. In the grave scenes, he is not only reformed rake and introspective lover, but also an embodiment of the ethical norm; likewise, in the gay scenes, he is not only true wit par excellence, but also the expositor of the norm and judge of deviations from the norm. In the grave scenes Mirabell is the norm for a morality worldly but wise; in the gay, for a wit brilliant but penetrating.

In the grave scenes the characters are not only mixed characters, compounded of potential and actual virtues and vices, but are also developing characters. Here Congreve contrasts a pair of adulterers who are more amenable to reformation with a pair who are less so. In the gay scenes, the witwouds are not only static characters, but their vices are more often affected than inherent. Here Congreve distinguishes between the character of a witwoud and a truewit; false wit, which is affected, is contrasted with true wit, which is indigenous. The difference between false and true wit is not primarily a difference of form, nor altogether one of content, it is fundamentally a difference in the degree of discrimination and judgment shown.

"Hasty judges" are perplexed by Congreve's witwoud because he is no longer the familiar Elizabethan, Jacobean, and earlier Restoration gull; he is no longer inarticulate, credulous, and simple-minded. Witwoud has come of age, he is no longer the gross and incorrigible fool driven by gullet and groin; he has blossomed into the affected and pretentious fool with agile tongue fed by retentive memory, grown so voluble, so arrogant, that careless critics accepting the witwoud at his own evaluation mistake him for a truewit. That this modification was intentional may be confirmed by recalling a passage in Congreve's dedication to *The Way of The World*:

Those characters which are meant to be ridiculed in most of our comedies, are of fools so gross, that, in my humble opinion, they should rather disturb than divert the well-natured and reflecting part of an audience; they are rather objects of charity than contempt; and instead of moving our mirth, they ought very often to excite our compassion.

This reflection moved me to design some characters which should appear ridiculous, not so much through a natural folly (which is incorrigible, and therefore not proper for the stage) as through an affected wit; a wit which at the same time that it is affected, is also false. (p. 313)

Why Congreve excludes the gross fool from comedy is clear from the passage quoted; what he means by affectation, and by implication, the affected fool, is apparent in the following excerpt from his letter to Dennis (1695), in which he describes affectation as a deliberate imitation of a selected model: "*Affectation*, shews what we would be, under a Voluntary Disguise. ... *Affectation* [is] from Industry. ... nothing is more common, that [sic] for some to affect particular ways of saying, and doing things, peculiar to others, whom they admire and would imitate."[11]

Congreve's affected fool is derived from Jonson's affected fools in the two humor comedies, *Cynthia's Revels* and *Epicoene*. Congreve, like Jonson, views affectation as a parasitic excrescence—born of self-love, bred by desire for eminence, fed by "stolen remnants," and restrained only by the ridicule of the truewit. The truewit in Congreve, as in Jonson, is conceived and portrayed as the ideal social and intellectual norm of the society of his era; the witwoud, the deviant from that norm; the truewit knows his own potentialities, limitations, and resources, and chooses to be himself; the witwoud willfully chooses neither to know himself nor to be himself, he strives to appear to be the truewit whom he admires and would imitate, hence witwoud escapes the realm of reason to roam in a world of fantasy. Pretense, invariably deliberate, occasionally naive, and frequently perverse, is the key to the psychology of affectation in both Jonson and Congreve. Both dramatists deride affectation because it frequently leads to malice and detraction, to words and deeds which are a source of misunderstanding, friction, and dissension.

Congreve's distinction "betwixt the character of a witwoud

and a truewit" [12] is demonstrably influenced by Ben Jonson, who developed a formula of expository satire in which a truewit is the agent, the witwoud the object, and an adaptation of the Theophrastan "character" the medium of satire. The character sketch as drawn by the truewit to stress the salient affectations of the witwoud is an effective dramatic device; it both anticipates and is later confirmed by the witwoud's own words and deeds; hence character sketch, dialogue, and action are interrelated, each throws light on the others; indeed, their very fusion seems to generate an expository satire which is comic as well as realistic.

Since the satiric "character" as Jonson and Congreve use it serves a function in comedy similar to that of soliloquy in tragedy, it has comparable validity. It is valuable also because the audience's first impression of the witwoud is not his "opinion" of himself; but is instead the judgment of a truewit, the very character best qualified to appraise folly and to ridicule affectation. The tempo of a comic episode accelerates when, immediately following a truewit's "portrait" of him, a witwoud enters, and by his own acts and words confirms the truewit's initial indictment.

Not in theory but in practice, Jonson first adumbrates the distinction between the "character" of a witwoud and a truewit in *Every Man in his Humour*, amplifies it in *Every Man out of his Humour*, expands it in *Cynthia's Revels*, and completes it in *Epicoene*. That Congreve had a detailed knowledge of these four comedies is apparent not only from echoes in *The Way of the World* itself but also from his letters to Dennis and Moyle.

Two letters [13] written in 1695, shortly after the success of *Love for Love*, indicate that Congreve had begun to conceive the idea of writing a comedy which like *Cynthia's Revels* would depict, expose, and deride contemporary humors and affectations, not necessarily those of the social climbers who traduce the court in Jonson's "Comical Satire" but rather those of the criticasters and poetasters who infect Will's coffee house:

I know not whether these Waters may have any communication with Lethe, but sure I am, they have none with the Streams of Helicon. I have often wondered how those wicked Writers of Lampoons, could croud together such quantities of execrable Verses, tagged with bad Rhimes, as I have formerly seen sent from this place: but I am half of Opinion now, that this Well is an Anti-Hypocrene. What if we should get a quantity of the Water privately conveyed into the Cistern at *Will's* Coffee-House, for an Experiment? But I am extravagant—Tho' I remember *Ben. Johnson* in his Comedy of CYNTHIA's *Revels*, makes a Well, which he there calls the *Fountain* of *Self-Love*, to be the Source of many entertaining and ridiculous Humours. I am of Opinion, that something very comical and new might be brought upon the Stage, from a Fiction of the like Nature. [14]

Later in this same letter, possibly reflecting on *The Poetaster* and *Bartholomew Fair* as well as *Cynthia's Revels*, Congreve continues speculating about the feasibility of reviving for his age the kind of comic satire on witwouds that Jonson had formerly contributed to the Jacobean era:

'Tis now the time, when the Sun breeds Insects; and you must expect to have the Hum and Buz about your Ears, of Summer Flies and small Poets. ... Methinks the Days of *Bartholomew-Fair* are like so many Sabbaths, or Days of Privilege, wherein Criminals and Malefactors in Poetry, are permitted to creep abroad. ... suffered to make abominable Mirth ... with vile Buffoonry. ...

A chatty letter sent in reply to Moyle's epistle of October 7, 1695, reiterates Congreve's contempt for the incredible cox-combry of the coffee-house "monsters":

There is no such Monster in this *Africa*, that is not sensible of your Absence; even the worst natured People, and those of least

Wit lament it, I mean, half Critics and Quiblers. ... I believe we may have variety of strange Animals, equal to *Paradise*, yet I fear we have not amongst us the *Tree of Knowledge*. It had been much to the disadvantage of Pliny, had the Coffee-house been in his Days; for sure he would have described some who frequent it, which would have given him the Reputation of a more fabulous Writer than he has now. But being in our Age it does him a Service, for us who know it, can give Faith to all his Monsters. [15]

At the height of his influence, Congreve writes to Keally (July 2, 1700): "You know I need not be very much alone; but I choose it, rather than to conform myself to the manners of my court and chocolate-house acquaintance." [16]

Congreve's Witwoud is the lineal descendant of his prototype, Fastidious Brisk, in *Every Man Out of His Humour*, and the technique for detraction follows the pattern set by the witwouds and collegiates in *Epicoene*. The salient affectations of both Witwoud and Brisk stem from their pretense to courtship and their pretense to wit. Both are fops—Fastidious subordinates his concern for courtship to his more ardent interest in apparel, Witwoud subordinates his concern for apparel to his intense desire to excel in repartee. Whereas to the former novel apparel is the "greatest good," to the latter a startling similitude begets the highest pleasure. Fastidious is charmed by similitudes uttered by others; Witwoud is so entranced by his own similitudes that he resents being interrupted by others. Both, like the critics of the "wit for wit's sake" school, regard wit and similitude as synonymous. Both assay repartee, although Brisk never achieves the vivacity and volubility of Witwoud. Both are double-dealers; both slander a friend behind his back, flatter him to his face.

Satirical character sketches of Witwoud are drawn by Mirabell and Fainall. Fainall describes Witwoud as having "something of good nature" and concedes he "does not always want wit," and Mirabell adds the finishing touches:

Mir. Not always: but as often as his memory fails him, and his common-place of comparisons. He is a fool with a good memory, and some few scraps of other folks' wit. He is one whose conversation can never be approved, yet it is now and then to be endured. He has indeed one good quality, he is not exceptious; for he so passionately affects the reputation of understanding raillery, that he will construe an affront into a jest; and call downright rudeness and ill language, satire and fire. (pp. 325–326)

Mirabell no sooner completes the portrait, than Fainall exclaims, "Behold the original!" and in minces Witwoud gasping "Afford me your compassion, my dears! pity me, Fainall! Mirabell, pity me!" Mirabell seizes this opportunity to verify his former remark that Witwoud "so passionately affects the reputation of understanding raillery, that he will construe an affront into a jest"; therefore, in response to Witwoud's "pity me," he gibes, "I do from my soul," and when Witwoud calls his own brother a fool, Mirabell in mock surprise protests, "A fool, and your brother," to which Witwoud indignantly rejoins, "... My half brother, he is, no nearer upon honour"; whereupon Mirabell ironically observes, "Then 'tis possible he may be but half a fool." (To Witwoud, snobbery, if not charity, begins at home.) When Witwoud complains, "my memory is such a memory," Mirabell warns, "Have a care of such apologies, Witwoud; for I never knew a fool but he affected to complain, either of the spleen or his memory" (pp. 326–327). Witwoud is incapable of distinguishing either between raillery and insult or between raillery and bickering. When Millamant accuses the witwouds of quarreling, he denies it with "Raillery, raillery, madam; we have no animosity—we hit off a little wit now and then, but no animosity.—The falling-out of wits is like the falling-out of lovers" (p. 363).

Besides pretending an understanding of raillery, Witwoud affects ease with women and proficiency in the invention of similitudes. The ladies reward his seeming affability by permitting him to share their scandal sessions. A satirical portrait which Witwoud draws and labels a lady of his acquaintance makes it apparent why he is invited to join the cabal; if he can concoct so fanciful a hyperbole about a mere mannerism, imagine how he might embellish an indiscretion: "... I know a lady that loves talking so incessantly, she won't give an echo fair play; she has that everlasting rotation of tongue, that an echo must wait till she dies, before it can catch her last words" (p. 347).

Act II, Scene 2, the initial entrance of Millamant, that famous scene so often quoted, illustrates Witwoud's resentment against Millamant because she will hardly allow anybody else wit; that a lady should love talking so incessantly that she won't give an echo fair play. Millamant has that everlasting rotation of tongue, she will talk, talk, talk, herself, yet ever say to the brisk spark at her side, a wit who can say as good things as ever she thought of, "truce with your similitudes; for I'm as sick of 'em—" (p. 345).

Witwoud, as a member of Lady Wishfort's cabal, has more frequent access to the company of Millamant than does Mirabell, who until the denouement is *persona non grata* both in her cabal and drawing room. However, the oftener Witwoud sees and particularly hears Millamant the more he resents her words and ways; indeed, he confides to Fainall precisely how he regards her and why: "Pshaw! pshaw! that she laughs at Petulant is plain. And for my part, but that it is almost a fashion to admire her, I should—hark 'ee—to tell you a secret, but let it go no further—between friends, I shall never break my heart for her. ... She's handsome; but she's a sort of an uncertain woman." Though she has wit, "'Tis what she will hardly allow anybody else:—now, demme, I should hate that, if she were as handsome as Cleopatra" (pp. 332–333).

Impressed by Witwoud's verve and volubility in the detraction scene, an unreflective audience or reader might assume that in this instance Witwoud belies his name. Here, stimulated by the leading questions of Fainall and Mirabell, he steals the scene; his wit appears to be too brilliant, his fancy too sustained to be labeled false wit. Here he himself when pointing out the shortcomings of Petulant lists many of the salient differences between true and false wit: "... if he had any judgment in the world, he would not be altogether contemptible"; he has "no more breeding than a bum-bailiff"; "in a controversy, he'll contradict anybody"; "he does not always think before he speaks;" "his want of learning"; "he never speaks truth."

Witwoud's wit is the quintessence of false wit; a line thinner than but as sharp as a rapier's edge separates his wit from true wit. In the following quotation, Witwoud's wit is false because it sacrifices loyalty to detraction; reason to casuistry. To elevate himself, he debases his friend; pretending to defend the character of Petulant, he besmirches it with calumny:

Mir. I don't find that Petulant confesses the superiority of wit to be your talent, Witwoud.

Wit. Come, come, you are malicious now, and would breed debates.—Petulant's my friend, and a very honest fellow, and a very pretty fellow, and has a smattering—faith and troth, a pretty deal of an odd sort of a small wit; nay, I'll do him justice. I'm his friend, I won't wrong him neither.—And if he had any judgment in the world, he would not be altogether contemptible. Come, come, don't detract from the merits of my friend.

Fain. You don't take your friend to be over-nicely bred?

Wit. No, no, hang him, the rogue has no manners at all, that I must own:—no more breeding than a bum-bailiff, that I grant you:—'tis pity, faith; the fellow has fire and life.

Mir. What, courage?

Wit. Hum, faith I don't know as to that, I can't say as to that— Yes, faith, in a controversy, he'll contradict anybody.

Mir. Though 'twere a man whom he feared, or a woman whom he loved.

Wit. Well, well, he does not always think before he speaks;—

we have all our failings: you are too hard upon him, you are, faith. Let me excuse him—I can defend most of his faults, except one or two: one he has, that's the truth on't; if he were my brother, I could not acquit him:—that, indeed, I could wish were otherwise.

Mir. Ay, marry, what's that, Witwoud?

Wit. O pardon me!—expose the infirmities of my friend!—No, my dear, excuse me there.

Fain. What, I warrant he's unsincere, or 'tis some such trifle.

Wit. No, no; what if he be? 'tis no matter for that, his wit will excuse that: a wit should no more be sincere, than a woman constant; one argues a decay of parts, as t'other of beauty.

Mir. Maybe you think him too positive?

Wit. No, no, his being positive is an incentive to argument, and keeps up conversation.

Fain. Too illiterate?

Wit. That! that's his happiness:—his want of learning gives him the more opportunities to show his natural parts.

Mir. He wants words?

Wit. Ay: but I like him for that now; for his want of words gives me the pleasure very often to explain his meaning.

Fain. He's impudent?

Wit. No, that's not it.

Mir. Vain?

Wit. No.

Mir. What! he speaks unseasonable truths sometimes, because he has not wit enough to invent an evasion?

Wit. Truths! ha! ha! ha! no, no; since you will have it,—I mean, he never speaks truth at all,—that's all. He will lie like a chambermaid, or a woman of quality's porter. Now that is a fault. (pp. 327–329)

Much as Plato would banish the fanciful poet from his *Republic* so would Hobbes shackle fancy in his *Leviathan;* not that either enjoys fancy less but that both admire judgment more. That fancy neither conforms with nor is bound by the laws of truth and reason is assumed by Hobbes, stated by Locke. Beginning with this premise, Locke concludes: "... it is a kind of affront to go about to examine it [fancy]."[17] To the contrary, Hobbes implies that unless fancy be confronted with judgment, man's ability to distinguish between good and evil, between appearance and reality, will be perverted, and consequently truth may become the vassal of beauty, reason, the pander of fancy. With these conflicting points of view in mind we propose to risk affronting Witwoud's fancy by confronting it with analysis:

The method of Witwoud's wit consists in a blurring of definitions, a juggling of ambiguities, and a reversal of values; the form is similitude, antithesis, aphorism, and hyperbole; the content, malice and detraction. Its surface brilliance obscures its shallowness; its seeming paradoxes are fraudulent. The wit is glib but giddy—buoyant, evanescent, and hollow as a bubble. The dizzy rapidity of his reversals of values is amusing but shallow. His vivacity coupled with his volubility blinds one to the extent he subordinates sense to sound. Under cover of a crescendo of hypnotic sound, fancy masks as judgment; opinion parades as reason. When values are implied, and since Witwoud is more literate than Petulant they occasionally are, they are capricious personal values, seldom traditional universal ones. His words are not the words of wit; they prostitute wit; his words are a gaudy substitute resembling wit, arrogantly parading as wit.

In controversies over the nature of wit there is agreement to this extent: wit is the index of an active and agile mind, a mind ready and able to conceive a fast succession of images and to combine them in telling comparisons—comparisons usually expressed as metaphor, similitude, or aphorism. However, in the major Restoration comedies by the leading dramatists, only witwouds equate wit with a bon mot and a similitude. Even Witwoud, who claims eminence as a contriver of similitudes, more frequently than not resorts to additional forms of figurative language, and the truewits use relatively few similitudes in proportion to the sort of tropes which express or heighten irony or satire. If one attempts to distinguish between the wit of a witwoud and a truewit solely on polish or on form, one will fail as "hasty judges" have failed from Congreve's time to our own; one must start anew, must see wit in action, must examine wit playing over a specific situation or relationship in a specific context. In *The Way of the World*, the masterly integration of form, content, and context determines the nature and quality of the wit, and furthermore, it is this threefold integration which in turn generates the more subtle forms of wit such as *double-entendre*, paradox, and dramatic irony.

Congreve's concept of true wit, like Jonson's, is a direct outgrowth of his staunch adherence to the dual function of comedy; that is why he insists that true wit both please and instruct, that true wit neither amuse at the expense of instruction; nor instruct at the expense of amusement. Only in true wit is the grace of fancy fused with the power of judgment; fancy enlivens and embellishes judgment, judgment directs and restrains fancy.

Petulant, town born, town bred, is a beau, a snob, and a pseudo cynic. He assumes he is a man of parts, but actually is a congenital fabricator and troublemaker. True to his name, and his name only, Petulant fretfully scrutinizes the world and its ways with a fixed and jaundiced eye; he sees and anatomizes the affectations and absurdities of others, but failing to turn his eye inward, he remains blind to his own follies. He is especially severe on Witwoud's shortcomings, and indulges in malice and detraction at his expense. As a snob, obsessed with a desire for eminence, he thrusts his person and patter into the company of the truewits. As a beau (cad), he brags of intimacies with prominent women of quality. Although the Ovidian code of seduction prescribes silence or denial to conceal an indiscretion, this vainglorious fop brags of enjoying favors which were never granted, by women he never met; he lies about women of quality, but lies with his own maid servant. Like Jonson's Fastidious Brisk, Petulant "swears tersely" and "cares not what lady's favor he belies."

The character of Petulant is contrasted in turn with that of Witwoud, who precedes him, and that of Sir Wilfull, who follows. Petulant is tenacious and contentious, whereas Witwoud is flighty and complaisant; Petulant affects a humor to contradict, whereas Sir Wilfull is afflicted with an ingrained humor of obstinacy. Petulant's affected humor is intentionally amorphous; to impress men, he chooses a humor to contradict; to startle women, a humor to be severe. Hoping to escape censure for flagrant violations of civility and breeding, he pretends his affected humor is a true humor, an instinctive drive over which he has no control, and for which he should not be held accountable. The "friendship" between Petulant and Witwoud is reminiscent of the same sort of disloyalty between Daw and LaFoole, and between the collegiates—all satirized at length in *Epicoene*.

The devices used to appear sought after recall Carlo Buffone's advice to Sogliardo in *Every Man in His Humour*. Witwoud betrays how his friend labors to acquire the appearance of popularity: "… why he would slip … out of this chocolate-house, just when you had been talking to him—as soon as your back was turned— whip he was gone!—then trip to his lodging, clap on a hood and scarf, and a mask, slap into a hackney-coach, and drive hither to the door again in a trice, where he would send in for himself; that I mean, call for himself, wait for himself; nay, and what's more, not finding himself, sometimes leave a letter for himself" (p. 330).

To Petulant, it is not enough that the ladies should appear to dog his footsteps, he must publicly flaunt the calculated cruelty beneath which they cringe. Fortunately for Petulant's enjoyment of his own ruse, he does not know that Witwoud has already confided to the company that the three "gentle women" of the brittle hearts are in reality naught but "two fasting strumpets, and a bawd … trulls whom he allows coach-hire, and something more, by the week, to call on him once a-day at public places"

(p. 329). After Petulant is urged to pacify the ladies in the coach, the pseudo gallant affects indifference, then calloused cruelty: 'Well, well;—I come.—'Sbud, a man had as good be a professed midwife, as a professed whoremaster, at this rate! to be knocked up and raised at all hours, and in all places. Pox on 'em, I won't come!—D'ye hear, tell 'em I won't come:—let 'em snivel and cry their hearts out" (p. 330). He then turns to the group of diverted gentlemen, leers, and affirms complacently, "I have a humour to be cruel" (p. 330). The wits pamper his absurd humor by asking flattering questions. Mirabell professes concern lest the victims may be persons of condition. Petulant boasts they are women of quality, adding, "Condition! condition's a dried fig, if I am not in humour!—By this hand ... they must wait or rub off, if I want appetite. ... let 'em trundle. Anger helps complexion, saves paint" (pp. 330–331).

Whereas the truewit feels obligated to protect the reputation of any woman he seduces, to challenge any aspersion of her character, to blot out, if need be, any defamation with the blood of the defamer; the witwoud attacks the reputation of women he pretends to have seduced, his fancy substitutes an imaginary for an actual consummation. So as long as Petulant's coach fantasy remains a fable, and the women involved are known harlots, little actual harm is done, and the fantasy may be accepted as a jest on the jester. When however, prompted by his humor to be severe, he shouts senseless ribaldry designed to humiliate unattended women strolling on the Mall, his aggressive insolence and ill breeding must be condemned.

Although Petulant prides himself on being popular with the ladies, he has to admit that Witwoud shares more in the secrets of the fair sex. He puts the situation in the best light possible by confiding that while Witwoud is favored most in public, it is Petulant whom the ladies favor in private. Proudly he boasts that women avoid him in public because they fear his malicious remarks. When Petulant professes himself in a humor to be severe,

Mirabell refuses to walk beside him, and furthermore expresses obvious contempt with the cad's way of exhibiting his severity:

Mir. ... walk by yourselves: let not us be accessory to your putting the ladies out of countenance with your senseless ribaldry, which you roar out aloud as often as they pass by you; and when you have made a handsome woman blush, then you think you have been severe.

Pet. What, what! then let 'em either show their innocence by not understanding what they hear, or else show their discretion by not hearing what they would not be thought to understand.

Mir. But hast not thou then sense enough to know that thou oughtest to be most ashamed thyself, when thou hast put another out of countenance?

Pet. Not I, by this hand!—I always take blushing either for a sign of guilt, or ill-breeding.

Mir. I confess you ought to think so. You are in the right, that you may plead the error of your judgment in defence of your practice.

> Where modesty's ill-manners, 'tis but fit
> That impudence and malice pass for wit. (p. 334)

In the preceding episode, after Mirabell invites Fainall to accompany him on a stroll through the park, Witwoud, himself uninvited, invites Petulant, and furthermore, suggests that he and his crony be severe especially at the expense of unaccompanied ladies who happen to be present. Only too familiar with the fops' customary behavior, Mirabell denounces Petulant's habit of forcing an unoffending woman to blush by assailing her with bawdry; and derides this habit for what it is, a premeditated display of gratuitous impudence and malice. Petulant attempts to shift the guilt from the attacker to the person attacked. Disregarding the point at issue, that a gentleman should refrain from gratuitous bawdry, he contends that if the lady were innocent, she would not understand his insult; if discreet, would ignore it. Mirabell reaffirms: a gentleman should be most ashamed himself when he has shamed another; a gentleman is never inadvertently rude; should he choose to be rude, he either must have adequate provocation or forfeit his claim to gentility. Still intent upon contradiction, Petulant airily insists that blushing indicates either guilt or ill breeding; whereupon Mirabell silences him with a ringing indictment of the pseudo cynic's manners, breeding, and judgment. The rhymed tag which terminates the first act is deliberately phrased to epitomize the licentious nature of false wit.

By discrediting impudence and malice, by identifying them with bad breeding and bad manners, Congreve makes truewit more responsible, more social, in the broadest sense of the word.[18] The truewit, not the witwoud, determines the degree of severity permissible to barb wit and make it sting. Manners, not as interpreted by critics but as understood and exemplified by the foremost Elizabethan and Restoration dramatists, are equated with morals; good manners are the external manifestation of humane instincts, propensities, and responses. The manners of a gentleman are gentle; the potential gentleness comes from heredity, is nurtured by education, is confirmed by habit, and is refined by association with his peers and betters.

The brace of town beaux, portrayed as fops, snobs, and bores, are egocentric exhibitionists avid for eminence. Since the witwoud neither knows himself nor wholly trusts himself, his arrogance is actually a sign of internal insecurity; hence he haunts the society and solicits the approbation of the truewit. The witwoud is vain, insistent, and loquacious; he knows no moderation, and resents all restraint. Even his display of pseudo wit is excessive; he indulges in hyperbole and draws a broad sword to decapitate a sparrow.

His fancy is intractable; it soars beyond the bounds of civility and good taste; it flouts accepted attitudes and standards; it violates modesty and good breeding. His vivid imagery, facile comparisons, and adroit juggling with ambiguities divert attention from the hollowness and brittleness of his wit. He flashes his wit as a tavern bully flourishes his sword, not to defend, but to offend. His wit is verbal anarchy—insolent, dissolute, and abandoned, it misrepresents characters, situations, and values. Readiness of evasion and waywardness of spirit drive his wit to excess; careless of his aim, he attacks the defenseless, the blameless, and even the praiseworthy. Ironically, he censors follies in others which frequently are more conspicuous in himself. At the height of his vainglory, Witwoud will tolerate a check from Mirabell, will accept insult for raillery, but when Millamant tends to pre-empt the wit, Witwoud impatiently orders her to desist, and Petulant silences her with vivid ribaldry. Frequently the witwoud prefers a monologue of his own to a dialogue of the truewits. Unrestrained fancy is invariably a social irritant; it defiles all it touches; as soon as aberrant fancy preys on values or ideals, they are altered, distorted, and degraded.

Originality, spontaneity, and appropriateness determine the quality of wit; false wit is borrowed, stolen, and inappropriate. For his "memorized scraps," the witwoud plunders the oral and written utterances of wiser and wittier men, and by tearing phrases from their context, he mutilates and degrades what he steals.[19] Since the witwoud's wit is mangled and secondhand, he becomes a mercer of small wit; the truewit finds the mercer and his wares equally offensive. Idle, vain, and callow, the witwoud thrusts his words and person where his presence is never sought, seldom approved, and reluctantly endured.

A number of key episodes have been interpreted, representative passages of dialogue quoted, and detailed analyses of wit in context presented—all indispensable preliminaries for a final summary of the distinction between the character of a witwoud and a truewit as developed by Congreve in *The Way of the World*.

The truewit commands wit of the highest order, truth old or new, stated with concise clarity in a perfect fusion of form and content. The truewit's is most frequently his own, derived from reading, observation, and reflection; whereas the witwoud's wit is inadvertently stumbled upon, borrowed without judgment, and memorized without reflection—scraps from plays, from commonplace books, and from the conversation of the truewits. The wit of the truewit is modified by civility, decorum, and discernment; the wit of the witwoud is frequently divorced from civility, decorum, and judgment. The truewit insists upon the sense and substance of wit, he, and he alone, can judge its quality and appropriateness; his control of wit is threefold, he is inventor, custodian, and judge. The witwoud chases the shadow of wit; his confident swagger comes from his very insecurity, he is forever courting the truewit's confirmation; he craves not wit but the reputation of being witty. The truewit's wit arises from self-knowledge, self-discipline, and self-assurance; the witwoud's from self-indulgence, self-aggrandizement, and self-delusion. The truewit's wit is social in nature, its twofold function is to entertain and to evaluate; the witwoud's wit is social only to the extent that his vanity needs and demands an attentive and applauding audience to his egoistic exhibitionism. Since the witwoud will sacrifice anybody or anything to arouse laughter, he is more frequently laughed at than with, and his presence is more often endured than enjoyed. Vulgarity, malice, and detraction taint the spirit of his wit. Wit, whether extemporaneous or borrowed and memorized, if divorced from civility, decorum, and judgment is the brand of the witwoud; never the hallmark of the truewit.[20]

Sir Wilfull comes fresh from the hinterlands with "no offence" driveling from his lips and reek of the stable still clinging to his boots. He is a lineal descendant of Sogliardo in *Every Man Out Of His Humour*. Like Sogliardo he is middle-aged, has left the country for a taste of London "lingo" and London delights, and bears with him into town the brand of rusticity—ignorance mingled with native shrewdness, crudity grounded in provincial habits, customs, and prejudices. He like his prototype is forced by social pressure to court a coquette who scorns him, and whose wit befuddles his wits. The differences between Jonson's and Congreve's boor are minor ones. Tutored by a rogue, Sogliardo apes fashionable attainments, affectations, and follies; Sir Wilfull first derides fashionable fops and fads, and then ineptly imitates them. At the time of his initial entrance every word and act of Sir Wilfull exude rusticity. The knight derides London beaux, belles, and breeding, since he is less at ease in a drawing room among his own relatives than in a tavern surrounded by hard liquor and easy wenches. As Fainall so aptly observes, "... when he's drunk he's as loving as the monster in the Tempest, and much after the same manner" (p. 325). In the drinking scene of Act IV, when wine makes him forget his alien environment, his tongue is loosened, his spirits rise, and he roars with anticipatory glee: "Ahey! wenches, where are the wenches? ... Is she a shakebag, sirrah? Let me bite your cheek for that" (p. 387). Forgetful of the slights of his coquettish cousin, of the tirades of his distracted aunt, and of the snubs and slurs of his half brother, this Caliban of the comedy of manners reels off in quest of wenches, bellowing as he reels, "'And a fig for your sultan and sophy'" (p. 387).

Hobbes's concept of sudden glory is exemplified in Act III, Scene 1, when the brace of town snobs endeavor to elevate themselves by degrading the alien from the country. Stalking him as if he were a monster, they examine and criticize his garments, his deportment, and his vernacular. The fraternal skirmish is a recognition episode in reverse, in which Witwoud exhibits the modish affectation of forgetting an uncouth relative, and Sir Wilfull, imitating the fop, professes an equally faulty memory. Pretending not to recognize his half brother, Witwoud inquires with mock surprise, "In the name of Bartlemew and his fair, what have we here?" (p. 364). Seeing Witwoud "so becravated, and so beperiwigged," Wilfull, who resents his garments and manners, in turn, remembers to forget a relative: "Hum! what, sure 'tis not

—yea by'r Lady, but 'tis—s'heart, I know not whether 'tis ... by the Wrekin. Brother ... i'faith! what, dost thou not know me? By'r Lady, nor I thee, thou art so becravated, and so beperi-wigged.—S'heart, why dost not speak? art thou overjoyed?" When Witwoud drawls, "Odso, brother, is it you? your servant, brother," the outraged knight sputters, "Your servant! why yours, sir. Your servant again ... and a—flap-dragon for your service, sir! and a hare's foot ... an you be so cold and so courtly." Witwoud mocks, "No offence, I hope, brother," and his choleric elder snaps, "but there is, and much offence!—A pox, is this your inns o'court breeding, not to know your friends and your relations, your elders and your betters?" Thereupon Witwoud condescends to explain, "... I tell you 'tis not modish to know relations in town: you think you're in the country, where great lubberly brothers slabber and kiss one another when they meet, like a call of serjeants—'tis not the fashion here. ..." Scornful of town breed-ing, the knight remarks, "The fashion's a fool; and you're a fop, dear brother," and therewith traces the decay of Witwoud's man-ners after having been infected by London:

S'heart, I've suspected this—by'r Lady, I conjectured you were a fop, since you began to change the style of your letters, and write on a scrap of paper gilt round the edges, no bigger than a *subpoena*. I might expect this when you left off, "Honoured broth-er;" and "hoping you are in good health," and so forth—to begin with a "Rat me, knight, I'm so sick of a last night's debauch"— 'ods heart, and then tell a familiar tale of a cock and a bull, and a whore and a bottle, and so conclude— (pp. 366–367).

With a candor seldom encountered except in one's kinsmen, Wilfull tells the company what a courteous and friendly lad Wit-woud had once been: "You could write news ... when you lived with honest Pimple Nose the attorney of Furnival's Inn—you could entreat to be remembered then to your friends. ..." (p. 367). Witwoud blazes with wounded vanity, Petulant guffaws with malicious delight, and rolls on his tongue bits of priceless information concerning the rustic and haphazard breeding of his affected and foppish companion.

Throughout Jacobean comedy, wit is the younger brother's weapon against the arrogance and despotism of his seniors; frequently the younger son is contending for his identity as an individual as well as for his share of worldly goods. In the country, the senior member of the family regardless of his intelligence or integrity governs the junior; away from his clan and his acres the elder shrinks in stature like those at Tunbridge-Wells "who at home converse only with their own Relations; and consequently when they come abroad, have few Acquaintance, but such as they bring with them."[21] In town, away from his former environment, youth challenges the wisdom and authority of age, disdains the ties of consanguinity, prefers as associates the friends and acquaintances of his own choice. Unfledged youth seeking liberty mistakes moderation for mediocrity, affectation for eminence, and railing for raillery.

Sir Wilfull cherishes his disgust with fashionable pretenses and affectations. Even the warm welcome extended by Lady Wishfort reminds him of the cool greeting of his brother. He grumbles, "I'm very well, I thank you, aunt. ... S'heart I was afraid you would have been in the fashion too, and have remembered to have forgot your relations. Here's your cousin Tony, belike, I mayn't call him brother for fear of offence" (p. 369). Soon the knight discovers his aunt also has been infected by city breeding, for when the maid informs her ladyship, "dinner is impatient," and the rustic with ale-house joviality remarks, "Impatient! why then belike it won't stay till I pull off my boots.—Sweetheart, can you help me to a pair of slippers?—My man's with his horses ..." his citified aunt chides, "Fy, fy, nephew! you would not pull off your boots here?—Go down into the hall ...." (p. 369).

Almost anyone except Lady Wishfort would perceive the futility of forcing a match between Millamant and Sir Willful; the pair are separated by breeding, taste, and background, as well as by precontract. Millamant's treatment of Sir Wilfull is intended not primarily to offend an unwelcome suitor but to forestall a proposal of marriage which she obviously cannot accept. (This is the only time Millamant attempts to overcome an obstacle in the way of her union with Mirabell.) Into the room in which Millamant is buried in revery, Mrs. Fainall thrusts Wilfull and locks the door. The bewildered boor attempts to begin a conversation; his greeting is the same one that Witwoud has used and Sir Wilfull had condemned as cold and courtly: "... your servant. No offence, I hope, cousin." Ignoring his presence, Millamant repeats lines from Suckling, commenting with approval, "... Natural, easy Suckling." Apparently "suckling" carries only barnyard or juvenile connotations for the rustic who protests, "Anan? Suckling! no such suckling neither, cousin, nor stripling: I thank Heaven, I'm no minor." Resenting that her pleasant fancies should be interrupted, she chides, "Ah, rustic, ruder than Gothic!" and the discomfited knight insists, "Well, well, I shall understand your lingo one of these days, cousin; in the meanwhile I must answer in plain English" (p. 376).

When in plain English she comes to the point, "Have you any business with me, Sir Wilfull?" he sheepishly meanders on toward the issue, "Not at present, cousin—yes I make bold to see, to come and know if that how you were disposed to fetch a walk this evening, if so be that I might not be troublesome, I would have sought a walk with you." Seeing him ill at ease, she heightens his discomfiture, "I nauseate walking; 'tis a country diversion; I loathe the country, and everything that relates to it" (implying including elderly and maladroit suitors). He shifts his ground, praises the town and its pastimes; she professes to hate the town as well; still he outstays his welcome, grows pseudophilosophical, "Dear heart, that's much—ha! that you should hate 'em both! ha! 'tis like you may; there are some can't relish the town, and others can't away with the country—'tis like you may be one of those, cousin." The boor remains impervious to the broad hint, "... You have nothing further to say to me?" dawdles on and on, until his cousin resorts to an abruptness little short of discourtesy, "If it is of no great importance ... you will oblige me to leave me. ..." (p. 377). He, no less befuddled than relieved, is shown the door, and lumbers out to herd with the males.

An appraisal of Congreve's satire in the courtship and "smoaking" episodes, long overdue, refutes the prevalent view that Congreve commends the sophistication of the town by deriding the stagnation of the country. Actually, his attitude is not partisan, but judicial; he approves neither place at the expense of the other; both places are conceived of primarily as environments; each is important only in relation to its impact on the growth or retardation of character; specific follies and vices, different but almost equally undesirable are indigenous to and prevalent in both; his derision of the environments is subordinated to his exposure of the follies and vices rife in each. Congreve unwaveringly holds the mirror up to nature:

So poets oft do in one piece expose.
Whole belles-assemblees of coquettes and beaux. (Epilogue)

The courtship episode may be seen as a boor's rebuff by a coquette, or as a contrast between country and town manners. It is both, but much more, the belle and the boor are satirized with almost equal severity. Congreve probes beneath breeding and manners to the psychology of character in action. Sir Wilfull's behavior is exhibited as crude, but Millamant's as rude. He at least has the excuse of ignorance of good breeding to condone his ill breeding; she, knowing how to be well-bred, chooses to be illbred. Owing to his limited background, he is instinctively ill at ease in her presence; instead of easing his embarrassment, she does all in her power to increase his abashment. Ever the coquette, she trifles even with an inept and an uncouth suitor; she forgets he is her kinsman and a human being, she treats him as if he were an alien and a buffoon.

The smoking episode is a contest between town arrogance and country shrewdness in which a brace of fops attack an alien from the hinterlands in a spirit suggestive of bearbaiting. Three comic reversals underscore its satiric irony: Witwoud, who instigated the attack, soon becomes the butt; Petulant, exulting in his former ally's discomfiture, joins the chorus of derision; whereupon the rustic knight shifts his attack from Witwoud's insolence to Petulant's disloyalty.

It is misleading to assume that all satire on vice is reserved for the grave scenes, or conversely, that all satire on folly is relegated to the gay scenes—Congreve is too astute a dramatist to draw so rigid a contrast. What he, like Jonson, does stress is that folly may deviate into vice; the fool may turn knave; or conversely vice may revert to folly, the knave may turn fool. But the implication is neither cynical nor pessimistic; it is rational and realistic. Knave and fool alike retain enough innate intelligence to be sensitive to ridicule, enough intelligence to be potentially corrigible, consequently after each has been shown the error of his ways, he may either mend them or go his perverse way. In comedy, as in life, knave or fool can be shown the way but he himself must choose whether to follow it.

Act IV, long as it is, seems short, since it spins at a dizzy pace set by the witwouds who, giddy with wine and self-love, cast off all affectations of breeding or civility, and revert to brag, brawl, and bicker. After the emotional tension of the highly charged altercation scenes with their grim emphasis on the aftermath of adultery, the fourth act with its hilarious succession of abortive and mock courtships, punctuated by two insolent proposals, speeds along on an air of uninhibited irresponsibility. The pervasive tone of high spirits and low morals is a perfect foil for the proviso scene, which looms as a reef of sanity elevated above the waves of indifferent, incongruous, and forced courtships. The grape releases the ape, the witwouds cavort and court, they swirl through Lady Wishfort's house and divert her from her anticipated reception of the proposal of the bogus Sir Rowland.

Drawn into the whirl of chaos, she pants and vociferates from chamber to chamber, pursuing the rioters, attacking them with tirades of invective. Finally checked by the summons of Sir Rowland, she recalls her opportunity and her suitor's ardor; thereupon, in a travesty of ceremonial language, she appeals to the gallantry of Witwoud:

Lady Wish. [*Aside to* Foible.]—Sir Rowland impatient? Good lack! what shall I do with this beastly tumbril?—[*Aloud.*] Go lie down and sleep, you sot!—or, as I'm a person, I'll have you bastinadoed with broomsticks.—Call up the wenches.

Sir Wil. Ahey! wenches, where are the wenches?

Lady Wish. Dear Cousin Witwoud, get him away, and you will bind me to you inviolably. I have an affair of moment that invades me with some precipitation—you will oblige me to all futurity. (pp. 386–387)

Congreve deliberately portrays this superannuated coquette as larger than life—as an elemental force fortified by paint, ratafia, and petticoats. He heightens her cyclonic invective, her contradictory and shifting aversions and diversions; her unquenchable lust for lust, power, and vengeance. Depicted as a humor character her manifold vices converge in a slough of iniquity: pride in her person, quality, and prejudices; envy of the youth, beauty, and charm of Millamant; wrath expressed in tirades against all who oppose her; lust on all levels, actual and imaginary; and avarice in her insistence on mercenary marriages between persons of incompatible temperaments.

Lady Wishfort's menage is a citadel of caprice, in which she is sovereign, Marwood her counselor, the witwouds her courtiers, and her daughter and niece captives. Critics see Millamant as fortune's favorite; actually she is fortune's hostage. As heiress with a known predispostion to disregard her guardian's authority, and even to sacrifice half her fortune in order to elope with the man of her choice, Millamant is suspect in the eyes of the cabal. After Lady Wishfort hears of and prevents the elopement, she founds the cabal, banishes Mirabell, and Millamant is left in an equivocal position, intolerable to one of her fastidious temperament. Lady Wishfort chooses to disregard the contract between the lovers; without Mirabell present to protect her, Millamant is subjected to the malice of the three women he has slighted (Lady Wishfort, Marwood, and Mrs. Fainall) and the humiliating courtship of the witwouds. During the Bacchanalia of Act IV, Millamant is assailed with proposals which run the gamut from the sagacious to the fatuous: Mirabell's provisos, she accepts; Petulant's, she disdains; Sir Wilfull's first proposal, she forestalls; and his second, evades.

Just as at the close of Act V, the predatory ruthlessness of the adulterers is exposed, so is the witwouds' uninhibited licentiousness unmasked at the close of Act IV, Scene 1. Stripped of pretensions and affectations, the witwouds throughout the Bacchanalia are held up to scorn as fools whose self-delusion has led to self-debasement. When Petulant's lewd fancy is heightened by wine, by an affected humor to be severe, and by an awareness of Millamant's equivocal position, he subjects her to an insolent proposal phrased in broad innuendo. Petulant, ever brazen, ever salacious, grows most offensive when he casually and abruptly demands the last favor. Millamant is stunned into silence; Witwoud, shocked into momentary sobriety, knows if Mirabell should hear of this insult a duel will ensue; but Petulant, deaf to shame, deaf to honor, leaves to consort with his maid:

Pet. You were the quarrel.

Mrs. Mil. Me!

Pet. If I have a humour to quarrel, I can make less matters conclude premises.—If you are not handsome, what then, if I have a humour to prove it? If I shall have my reward, say so; if not, fight for your face the next time yourself—I'll go sleep.

Wit. Do, wrap thyself up like a wood-louse, and dream revenge—and hear me, if thou canst learn to write by to-morrow morning, pen me a challenge.—I'll carry it for thee.

Pet. Carry your mistress's monkey a spider!—Go flea dogs, and read romances!—I'll go to bed to my maid. (p. 384)

Lady Wishfort, surrounded by daughter, niece, and nephew, secure and confident in her sanctum of pseudo sophistication, is determined to perpetrate the mercenary marriage of her fastidious niece to her besotted nephew. This incongruous match was first suggested to the guardian by Marwood, who, slighted by Mirabell and taunted by Millamant (III, 3), seeks revenge against both offenders; her attempt to yoke her rival with a rustic boor is intended to deprive Mirabell of the heiress and her fortune. When the incendiary first suggested the match, her patroness was inclined to reject the idea; in a moment of caprice, she accepted it; and finally became obsessed with its desirability. Preoccupied with anticipation of her own courtship, distracted by Sir Wilfull's "rantipole clamour," fearing that Millamant will not be induced to agree to the match until the "Borachio" has been refined by travel, the guardian resorts to casuistry in glossing over her nephew's defects:

Sir. Wil. S'heart, an you grutch me your liquor, make a bill—give me more drink, and take my purse. ... But if you would have me marry my cousin—say the word, and I'll do't—Wilfull will do't. ...

Lady Wish. My nephew's a little overtaken, cousin—but 'tis with drinking your health.—O' my word you are obliged to him.

Sir Wil. *In vino veritas*, aunt.—If I drunk your health to-day, cousin—I am a Borachio. But if you have a mind to be married, say the word, and send for the piper; Wilfull will do't. ... (p. 385)

Millamant undergoes a final ordeal when between health in bumpers, the "Borachio" relapses into the vernacular of doxy courtship: "... if I had a bumper, I'd stand upon my head and drink a health to 'em.—A match or no match, cousin with the hard name?—Aunt, Wilfull will do't. If she has her maidenhead, let her look to't; if she has not, let her keep her own counsel in the meantime, and cry out at the nine months' end" (p. 386).

Indifferent to the sordidness of Sir Willfull's courtship, his aunt berates him, not because he is a sottish vulgarian, but because he has revealed his character before Millamant has agreed to marry him! Nevertheless, the guardian assumes time and travel will polish his crudities and make him an acceptable groom. Still resentful that her nephew's match must be delayed, Lady Wishfort hastens to fulfill her fantasies of courtship with the bogus Sir Rowland. The flamboyant courtship of Sir Rowland surpasses her ladyship's most rhapsodic anticipations; in a travesty of gallantry, he pledges himself ready and able to satisfy her ardor, her vengeance, and her avarice. Anyone familiar with this memorable mock courtship will recall the inimitable exchange of compliments, assurances, and commitments—the sustained hypocrisy—vulgar, spontaneous, and somehow pathetic. Delusions of grandeur, so fatuously senile, so patently absurd—aberrant fancy's last shift to compensate for the slights of fortune and the ravages of time.

In *The Way of the World*, behavior is based on and judged by principles, not on proverbs nor copy-book maxims; hence the morality reflects those permanent and universal values which civilized man, regardless of creed or country, has promulgated and cherished. Showing no traces of sentimentality, satire is unflinchingly rational in its exposure and indictment of affectation, eccentricity, dissimulation, and sophistry.

A recurrent problem in Restoration comedy, which probably disturbed Wycherley more profoundly than it did either Etherege or Congreve, was how to establish and convey an impression of a mean between the plain dealer and the double-dealer, especially after the traditional Jonsonian demonstrator had been either modified beyond recognition or totally discarded. Congreve's solution in his last comedy was to depict the *savoir-faire* of the truewit as a norm, midway between the gratuitous asperity of the plain dealer and the calculated hypocrisy of the double-dealer. Since the excess of asperity leads to folly, the excess of hypocrisy, to knavery, neither plain dealer nor double-dealer is a suitable norm for realistic comedy; indeed, only the truewit is sufficiently balanced and resourceful to cope with those peculiarities of behavior which set one man too far apart from his fellows for the well-being of either. The approved mores, in this comedy, depend on a policy of laissez faire for those capable of self-direction, one of coercion for those incapable of self-discipline; the truewit, as an accredited representative of the group, restrains wayward egos from expanding beyond the predetermined limits regarded as socially and morally acceptable. After the distinction between the truewit and a witwoud is clarified, the nature of the norm determined, and the relation of corrigibility to the regeneration-degeneration motif understood, this conclusion, surprising though it may seem, emerges: the ethos of Congreve's most mature and reflective comedy is essentially conventional; it is the morality of the golden rule, modified by the principle of the golden mean.

In this comedy, the tantalizing fascination of Congreve's wit lies in its range, its variety, and its incomparable subtlety. To appreciate these three qualities, one must not be diverted from the sense by the sound, one must pierce the form to grasp the thought, and above all, one must be aware that Congreve reveals wit in act as well as in word. The wit of Congreve is a polished flexible instrument capable of anatomizing a wide range of attitudes and emotions. The source of the wit is the reaction, emotional or intellectual, to the conflict between appearance and reality, reason and instinct, civility and caprice, breeding and vulgarity, and morality and hypocrisy. Wit is seldom an end in itself; it serves an end greater than itself. The quality of the wit is determined by the emotional and intellectual integrity of the mind from which it emanates. Witwouds usually speak and act foolishly; knaves usually speak and act licentiously; and the true wits, and only the true wits, usually speak and act judiciously. An awareness of the psychological interplay of wit, emotion, and action makes it possible to see how any one or any combination of these three may be either cause or effect in a closely integrated cycle of reaction. Or to amplify, true wit, as Congreve employs it, is seldom solely verbal; it carries through will into act; or into either mutual concessions or further conflict when all implications of the act contemplated or consummated have been weighed. Whenever wit (judgment) weighs or copes with consequences, moral choice is demanded, since the character must choose the extent to which he will accept or evade the consequences of his own way of life.

Seen in the perspective of Congreve's development, each of his last three comedies is an increasingly successful attempt to revive, to reaffirm, and to demonstrate the depth, the range, and the power of satiric comedy. A chronological survey of the prologues to Congreve's plays shows that although he consistently courts his audience's favor, he grows increasingly conscious that as the accredited successor to Ben Jonson and Wycherley, satire is his rightful inheritance. So, paradoxical though it seems, he craves the approval of an audience which resents satire, yet refuses to cater to the public taste by refraining from satire; he seems torn between a knowledge of what constitutes profitable dramatic practice and an urge to reinstate the dual function of comedy. He, like his most distinguished pre-Restoration predecessors, is convinced that "exalted" comedy should instruct as well as delight.

The prologue to his first play is little more than a novice's plea for indulgence, adroitly expressed in antithetical similitudes. After the phenomenal success of *The Old Bachelor*, the poet boldly presented *The Double-Dealer* to his public. The confidence of the young dramatist was rudely shaken; upon first representation *The Double-Dealer* was coldly received. Not until after Dryden generously pointed out its merits did the comedy become popular:

> In him all beauties of this age we see,
> Etherege his courtship, Southerne's purity;
> The satire, wit, and strength of manly Wycherley.

Still smarting from the initial reception of his previous play, Congreve, in his prologue to *Love for Love*, berates cowardly poets and conceited audiences, expresses the desire "to lash this crying age," then lest his hearers be offended by such presumption, assures them that his satire will be restrained by good manners:

> Though 'satire scarce dares grin, 'tis grown so mild,
> Or only shows its teeth as if it smiled.
> As asses thistles, poets mumble wit,
> And dare not bite, for fear of being bit.
> . . . .
> Since *The Plain Dealer's* scenes of manly rage,
> Not one has dared to lash this crying age.
> This time the poet owns the bold essay,
> Yet hopes there's no ill-manners in his play.

Five years after the triumph of *Love for Love*, *The Way of the World* was staged. In its prologue Congreve attempts to beguile his spectators into approving satire. With witty ambiguity he pretends his sole purpose is to delight, then slyly begs his audience's indulgence should he inadvertently expose vice or folly, assuring his listeners with ironic gravity nobody present can be offended since "so reformed a town" harbors neither knave nor fool:

To please, this time, has been his sole pretence,
He'll not instruct, lest it should give offence.
Should he by chance a knave or fool expose,
That hurts none here, sure here are none of those.

The quotations appearing on the title pages of Congreve's comedies are valuable guides for interpretation. The lines from Horace's satire suggest the theme, plot, and character of the principal protagonists of *Love for Love;* the quotation from Horace's *Ars Poetica,* "Nevertheless, sometimes even comedy exalts her voice," suggests the tone of the grave scenes of *The Double-Dealer;* and that from Terence, "... I can deceive them both by speaking the truth," epitomizes both the character and the *modus operandi* of the double-dealing antagonist; taken together the two quotations emphasize Congreve's intent to reinstate the dual purpose of comedy, by subordinating satire on folly to satire on vice. Contrary to current practice, Congreve did attempt, in *The Double-Dealer,* to combine sustained satire on vice with sustained satire on folly. This attempt evoked technical problems more numerous and more complex than he was able to resolve at this stage of his development.

The plot of *The Double-Dealer* is even more shifting and more complex than that of *The Way of the World;* asides and soliloquies are employed to excess; motivation is frequently perplexing because there is too wide a gap between the intelligence of Mellefont and that of Maskwell; and Mellefont is too credulous to represent a norm, whereas Maskwell and Lady Touchwood are too vicious for comedy. The spirit of the gay scenes is permeated with *carpe diem* attitudinizing; that of the grave scenes tainted with melodramatic intrigue, hysterical emotion, and sudden violence more suggestive of heroic tragedy than satiric comedy. Because there is too tenuous an integration between the gay scenes, which ridicule folly, and the grave scenes, which expose vice, *The Double-Dealer* was a dramatic and aesthetic failure—but a magnificent failure, a failure which contributed much more to Congreve's development as a reflective dramatist than did the phenomenal success of his first play, *The Old Bachelor*.

In devising the plot for *Love for Love*, Congreve adapted the pattern of the "honest" hoax used successfully by Middleton in *A Trick to Catch the Old One*, and Massinger in *A New Way to Pay Old Debts*. Middleton's Witgood and Massinger's Wellborn are two important examples of a prodigal turned constant lover, comparable in many respects to Valentine in *Love for Love*. In all three comedies, the prodigal's reformation is described in retrospective dialogue as having taken place before the play begins; the regeneration of the protagonist is traced through an intrigue designed to regain or to retain a legacy out of which the wastrel has been or is about to be swindled. Contrary to the practice of Middleton and Massinger, and to his own practice in *The Way of the World*, Congreve in *Love for Love* did not subordinate love to the intrigue based on the retention of the legacy.

The honest hoax rises out of the struggle between youth and age over the possession of inherited wealth; the "honest" hoax almost invariably violates the letter but champions the spirit of the law. Its morality is a relative not an absolute one; it is a hoax to rectify a swindle. Its spirit is indigenous to and appropriate for intrigue comedy wherein witty youth contends with knavish age to regain or to retain material possessions.

The typical pattern of intrigue centered on the honest hoax develops as follows: an experienced extortionist encourages an inexperienced wastrel in his prodigality by providing ready money on seemingly easy terms, and demands in return some sort of legal document as security. After discovering that he has been duped into signing an extortionate document, the prodigal, in desperation, strikes back through an adroitly designed hoax keyed to trap the extortionist through his avarice. Hence the deceiver is deceived partly through his own dominant weakness, which makes him receptive to the hoax, and partly by the wit of the wastrel, who designs and carries out the hoax.

The prodigal's hoax is accepted as an "honest" hoax for two reasons: First, the prodigal finds himself in a situation where there is no legal redress; second, it is axiomatic that the prodigality or licentiousness of youth is less vicious and more corrigible than the predatory avarice of age.

In *The Double-Dealer*, Congreve experiments with a multiplex[22] plot; in *Love for Love* he perfects it; this three- or more ply arrangement eliminates subplots by substituting in their stead parallel intrigues carried on by subsidiary characters who sometimes impede, other times accelerate the focal conflict between the leading protagonist and antagonist. The plot of *Love for Love* is ingeniously composed of three sharply differentiated but reciprocally interdependent strands: the first strand, the prodigal's pursuit of the heiress, is more romantic than realistic; the second, the father-son inheritance conflict, is in turn materialistic, philosophic, and satiric; and the third, a sequence of cross-wooing, is realistic and satiric.

Unpaid debts and unrequited love disturb the hero almost equally; to prevent his father from disinheriting him, and to induce Angelica to reveal her love, Valentine feigns madness; the rumor of his insanity sets off an exciting sequence of antagonisms and alliances which continue well into the fifth act. The prodigal's scheme to retain the inheritance which he has signed an agreement to relinquish is an adaptation of the honest hoax of Middleton and Massinger. In this comedy, as in *The Way of the World*, two legal documents are involved; in *Love for Love* the initial document is an acknowledgment that, in return for four thousand pounds received to pay his creditors, Valentine is bound to sign a second document which will irrevocably convey his birthright to his brother.

The legacy conflict is prominent in the plots of the most frequently performed and best-attended seventeenth-century comedies; beginning in *The Double-Dealer*, continuing in *Love for Love*, and culminating in *The Way of the World*, Congreve stresses and deepens the cultural implications of this conflict. As observed in nature, as taught by church, as established by law, the father-son relationship is traditionally regarded as inviolable; in nature it may be impulsively hostile, but both church and law restrain impulse by specifying mutual obligations intended to be mutually beneficial. During the legacy-conflict in *Love for Love*, not only does the customary protector turn predator, but in so doing attempts to circumvent the law of primogeniture, the very cornerstone of a class-conscious society whose continued existence is dependent upon the law of hereditary succession. Congreve develops a sequence of impressive scenes out of the inheritance conflict, two of which are unique in Restoration comedy: the first (II, 1), a lively, intense, and strangely moving altercation scene; the second (IV, 2), an ingeniously satiric and philosophic scene of feigned madness. In the first episode, the dramatist contrasts the humanism of the resentful son with the materialism of the despotic father through a sustained and passionate contest of wit and will as each argues his concept of the respective prerogatives and responsibilities of sire and heir. In the second, to delay signing the inheritance transfer, the heir deliberately oscillates between apparent sanity and seeming insanity; and by adroitly timing his lucid intervals to coincide with the absence of Buckram succeeds not only in convincing the lawyer that Valentine is *non compos mentis* and unqualified to sign, but also in frustrating his father, who is certain but unable to prove that his son's madness is counterfeit. During this episode, the turns and twists of the intrigue provoke dialogue which explores the hidden recesses of mind and heart; dialogue in which the serio-comic implications are universal.

In the second plot strand, the report that Valentine is about to sign away his inheritance and later the rumor that his madness will enable him to retain his legacy set off a complicated sequence of incongruous and mercenary marriage proposals. For various and mixed motives, most of them sordid—superstition, lust, caprice, spite, reputation, or lucre—a sequence of eight alliances are proposed and broken with giddy rapidity. The Frail sisters dissolve the Ben-Prue (1) arrangement of the oldsters by encouraging in its stead a Prue-Tattle (2) flirtation and a Frail-Ben (3) courtship. Not until after Sir Sampson threatens to disinherit Ben, does Frail scheme to discard Ben and trap in his place the "mad" Valentine as mate (4).

In addition to the four proposed matches which have been mentioned, two equally or perhaps more absurd couplings are suggested—Tattle-Angelica (5) and Prue-Robin (6). A seventh, Sir Sampson-Angelica, is developed in greater detail to resolve the impasse brought about by Valentine's feigned incapacity to sign the inheritance transfer. Not one of these seven volatile couplings terminates in matrimony; in most cases, the motives underlying the match have been sordid, the intrigues capriously started and whimsically dropped; frequently the duper in turn becomes the duped; the intrigue which begins as cross-wooing ends as cross-overreaching. Finally, however, one couple is legally yoked, when, to inflict the meddlers on each other, Valentine devises a masked marriage of Frail to Tattle. The traditional masked marriage, in this instance, is not as trite a device as is commonly assumed; Tattle and Frail are victimized more by their own cupidity and gullibility than by the chicanery of master and servant; ironically their own folly induces them to accept speed, secrecy, and the disguises of friar and nun.[23]

In addition to the eight couplings which lead to lively intrigue, animated dialogue, and urbane satire, two seduction episodes in the sprightliest *carpe diem* vein add to the levity of this realistic strand. The Prue-Tattle seduction is on the verge of consummation when accidentally interrupted by the nurse; the more sophisticated Scandal-Mrs. Foresight seduction is consummated, but when at next encounter his partner in dalliance gives Scandal reason to wonder whether he was the seducer or the seduced, his conquest becomes Pyrrhic.

Not only is the licit and illicit intrigue shifting and intricate, but the expressed views of the intriguers are sufficiently varied to represent the conflicting philosophies prevalent in contemporary society: Foresight, haunted by horns, is petulant and superstitious; Jeremy, a Latinate witty servant, is rational and realistic; Prue, the romp with an itch for wedlock, is impulsive and sensual; Sir Sampson, Ben, and the nurse, in varying degrees, are vulgar, opinionated, and materialistic; and the Frail sisters and Scandal (wanton wife, cast mistress, and facile rake), are licentious and cynical.

The inherently incompatible marriages proposed by this group are ubiquitous in Restoration comedy; the sort which not only lead to friction, satiety, and adultery but also to bawdy innuendo and epigrammatic cynicism directed at the galling weight of the marital yoke. In speech after speech, in successive comedies, Congreve points out that not marriage but the character of those who marry is at fault. Jealous husband, erotic wife, glib rake, petulant oldster, silly romp, giddy flirt, and brisk witwoud alike are poor matrimonial risks; they degrade marriage from a sacrament to a legal bond used to defraud and to despoil. Avarice, malice, and dissimulation destroy the validity of any permanent or intimate relationship. Capricious yet obstinate, these moral mavericks snatch at lust since they are so impatient, so unstable, so egocentric that they are neither capable of loving nor worthy of being loved.

Technically, the two realistic plot strands are enveloped by the romantic strand with which the play opens and closes and from which the comedy derives its title. The spirit of Valentine's pursuit of Angelica, with which the play begins, and her surrender, with which it ends, is predominantly romantic, although it occasionally oscillates between the satiric and the sentimental. The spirit of absolute and reciprocal love characteristic of the love-for-love strand contrasts with the marriage à la mode tone of the satiric strand. Although the reforming prodigal and the

skeptical heiress do share an equally reflective and idealistic concept of love and marriage, she has just cause to doubt, and ability
to try his fidelity, probity, and veracity. At the outset he declares
his love, whereas she, more wary, tests and retests the sincerity
of his protestations until, finally believing he has lost his bride,
Valentine volunteers to sign the inheritance transfer. This romantic gesture convinces Angelica that his love is unalloyed and
manifestly free from a mercenary taint. The sincerity, constancy,
and generosity displayed by the hero, and increasingly felt and
finally expressed by the heroine, fuse into an idealism which not
only contrasts with but also counterbalances the impact of cynical
materialism expressed and illustrated in the two realistic strands.

To refute Collier's charge that such debauched sparks as Valentine are rewarded with wives and fortunes in the last act,
Congreve, aware that not only the character of his protagonist
but also his seeming violation of poetic justice is being attacked,
replies at some length:

Valentine is in *Debt*, and in *Love;* he has honesty enough to close
with a hard Bargain, rather than not pay his Debts, in the first
Act; and he has Generosity and Sincerity enough, in the last *Act*,
to sacrifice every thing to his Love; and when he is in danger of
losing his Mistress, thinks every thing else of little worth. This,
I hope, may be allow'd a Reason for the Lady to say, *He has
Vertues*: They are such in respect to her; and her once saying so,
in the last *Act*, is all the notice that is taken of his *Vertue* quite
thro' the Play.

Mr. *Collier* says, he *is Prodigal*. He was Prodigal, and is shewn,
in the first *Act* under hard Circumstances, which are the Effects
of his Prodigality. ... In short the Character is a mix'd Character;
his Faults are fewer than his good Qualities; and, as the World
goes, he may pass well enough for the best Character in a Comedy;
where even the best must be shewn to have Faults, that the best
Spectators may be warn'd not to think too well of themselves.[24]

Congreve's vindication of Valentine is also a defense of the ethos in *Love for Love;* hence a restatement of the points enumerated and implied seems appropriate: since the protagonist has been a prodigal, he is shown suffering the consequences of his prodigality even after he has begun to reform; since the nature of comedy proscribes flawless characters, the hero is presented as a mixed character whose good qualities are more numerous than his bad; since the purpose of comedy is to instruct as well as to amuse, a dramatist must depict the absurdities of human frailty to remind his audience that self-appraisal is a safeguard against self-adulation.

Guided by a finer sense of selection and subordination, a more incisive theory of wit, a deeper understanding of the nature and purpose of comedy, and a firmer concept of an appropriate ethos for exalted comedy, Congreve created *The Way of the World*, his greatest ethical as well as aesthetic achievement. In place of the *carpe diem* episodes which fill so many pages of the second, third, and fourth acts of *Love for Love*, Congreve in *The Way of the World* presents the diversions of the irrepressible Lady Wishfort, the satiric incidents exposing open and covert detraction, and the unique episodes which distinguish between the character of a witwoud and a truewit. Unlike the Valentine-Angelica courtship, which is carried into and becomes part of the love-lucre conflict resolved in a somewhat abortive denouement, Mirabell and Millamant come to terms in the fourth act, thus freeing the fifth act for a sustained legacy conflict between the four adulterers, a conflict throughout which imminent victory shifts from side to side until the valid deed of conveyance assures both a realistic denouement, and an "artful solution of the *fable*."

The ethos of the last two comedies is centered on the contrast between the protagonists' regeneration and the antagonists' degeneration; in each instance the leading protagonist is generous and introspective, the foremost antagonist predatory and opportunistic. Since, as Congreve interprets him, Aristotle restricts the subject matter of comedy to "the Vices most frequent, and which are the common Practice of the looser sort of Livers," it seemed to follow that virtuous deeds or characters should be excluded from comedy. On the other hand, since "poets are instructed, and instruct; not alone by precepts which persuade, but also by examples which illustrate,"[25] it appears that the dramatist must both prescribe and depict virtue. Thus, since the nature of comedy demands the portrayal of only foolish and vicious characters, whereas the purpose of comedy seemingly requires the representation of wise and good characters, the dramatist is faced with a technical dilemma. This problem Congreve solved by reviving the Middleton and Massinger sort of mixed character, a protagonist who is neither wholly good nor wholly evil, neither entirely wise nor entirely foolish. The hero of Congreve's third play is a reforming prodigal; the norm of the fourth, a reforming rake; the concept of a mixed character reinforced by the theory of corrigibility enabled Congreve not only to prescribe but also to represent the reformation of a formerly licentious character.

Plagued by bantlings, creditors, imminent incarceration, a gibing servant, a cynical ally, an elusive inamorata, and a tyrannical father—little wonder that Valentine is neither as active in intrigue, as rational in argument, nor as balanced in crises as Mirabell. The sudden reformation of Valentine, and especially of Scandal, is more rhetorical and less convincing than the more slowly developed and well-motivated reclamation of Mirabell and Mrs. Fainall. The fifth-act conversion of the rake and the prodigal in *Love for Love* is too impulsive, and too perfunctory; it represents not final restraint, but the substitution of one form of excess for another; whereas the gradual regeneration of the former rake and his cast mistress stems from an acceptance of a social and ethical norm through which they achieve self-knowledge and self-mastery.

In *Love for Love*, the conflict over the legacies of Valentine, Angelica, and Prue has a blurred triple focus, because even though

the protagonists usually remain the same individuals, the antagonists vary; the conflict between father and son alternately
separates from and merges with the conflict between the romantic
lovers, as well as with the conflict between the marriage specu-
lators. Not only is there conflict within the separate strands, but
also conflict between the separate strands; consequently integration is achieved at the expense of adequate subordination. In
The Way of the World, the fixed conflict is focused on the conten-
tion between a pair of protagonists and a pair of antagonists for
the control of Lady Wishfort's disposal of the three legacies.
Compared with the denouement and conclusion of *The Way of the
World*, the sequence of surprises and reversals which continue well
into the fifth act of *Love for Love*, though exciting theater, are
inferior dramaturgy.

In the fifth act of *Love for Love*, the impact of two active
counterintrigues on one passive intrigue produces a diffuse conflict which increases the status of Sir Sampson and of the heroine
by decreasing that of the hero. Valentine's counterfeit madness,
devised as passive resistance to deadlock his father's coercive
tactics, has created an impasse which Angelica breaks in the
denouement by provoking Valentine's romantic gesture. During
her final impassioned indictment of the father's pettiness and
praise of the son's generosity, she extols true love which conquers
all obstacles. Though, for Angelica, love must be absolute and
undefiled, the way she prevents the father from obtaining the
son's inheritance is sufficiently devious to cope with human
frailty. Angelica's trick to catch the old one—her pretense of
preferring the father to the son as mate, her flattery of the oldster's
virility boasts, her seeming readiness to accept as jointure a legacy
rightfully belonging to his son, her tearing the bond inimicable to
her lover's welfare—may be justified as relative morality, and her
behavior be condoned as fit for an 'honest" hoax devised to prevent a legalized swindle.

There is a significant, though seldom if ever quoted, remark in

Congreve's *Ammendments of Mr. Collier's False and Imperfect Citations. ...* : "Mr. *Collier* has indeed given me an opportunity of reforming many Errors, by obliging me to a review of my own Plays."[26] Perhaps it was this review which made Congreve sufficiently aware of "errors" in his earlier plays to avoid them in his last; perhaps it was wider reading, increased assimilation, and intenser reflection on playwriting which refined his craftsmanship and deepened his insight into man and society. Regardless of the cause, *The Way of the World* is the supreme example of the exalted comedy which Congreve avowedly attempted but failed to achieve in *The Double-Dealer*. Not only is the regeneration-degeneration motif pivotal in the ethos of Congreve's last two comedies, but also his concept of morality is regulated and his creative process directed by these four convictions: that the interplay of instinct and reason is conditioned by the nexus of past, present, and future; that the affected fool, not the gross and incorrigible fool, is suitable for satiric comedy; that true wit, judgment, and morality are reciprocally interdependent; and finally that within man himself lies the power to improve his potential aptitudes and capacities.

Reflective critics accept the belief, which poets and philosophers have reiterated from time immemorial, that no art will endure, nor deserves to endure, unless it embodies a quest for truth. Since drama imitates character in action, and since the impact of art is heightened by moderate exaggeration, characters in drama are frequently depicted as somewhat better or somewhat worse than people in real life; tragedy tends to depict man as nobler than he is; comedy, as baser. If, with Jonson and Congreve, one accepts the dual function of comedy, both to please and instruct, one may understand how pleasure is roused through insight into man's moral, mental, and emotional bents. Congreve communicates this insight by skill in consistent and sound characterization and motivation, by ingenious presentation of comic incident, by mastery of figurative language, by such technical devices as tests, provisos, altercations, suspense, surprise, discovery, and reversal. Laughter, in turn, is aroused by the sudden exposure of trivial, false, or distorted values, or by unmasking affectation, stupidity, or viciousness. Hence, regardless of whether or not poetic justice is awarded in the fifth act, comedy, like tragedy, has a cathartic value; for comedy, by depicting error, unmasks error; pointed wit strips the veils of illusion from evil and exposes both folly and vice to ridicule.

"Congreve's muse is the full-blooded jade of Etherege and Wycherley come to discretion," asserts John Palmer.[27] If Congreve's muse be a jade, and there is much evidence to the contrary, she has become not merely discreet, but regenerate; not wary, but wise; less concerned with appearance than reality; less with casuistry than truth. In the denouement and conclusion of such comedies as *Volpone* and *The Way of the World*, exalted comedy hovers at the brink of tragedy, because as Jonson himself saw, "the moving of laughter [is not] always the end of comedy."[28] At its height, Congreve's satire goes beyond the exposure of vice, beyond the indictment of evil, and reveals glimpses of ultimate good in a spirit akin to tragic catharsis.

The Way of the World is a reflective play written by a dramatist who, like Ben Jonson, thinks of himself as a poet; of a poet as a "maker or, a feigner" who forms a fable which imitates truth; of the fable as "the form and soul" of drama; of comedy at its best as an exalted form of poetry; and of poetry as sovereign of the arts.[29] Seldom, if ever, does Congreve write with more fervent sincerity than when in his dedication to *The Way of the World* he reaffirms the basic tenets of Ben Jonson's aesthetic creed:

Little of it [this play] was prepared for that general taste which seems now to be predominant in the palates of our audience. ... It is only by the countenance of your Lordship; and the *few* so qualified, that such who wrote with care and pains can hope to be distinguished; for the prostituted name of *poet* promiscuously levels all that bear it ... some of the coarsest strokes of Plautus, so

severely censured by Horace, were more likely to affect the multi-
tude; such who come with exception to laugh at the last act of
a play, and are better entertained with two or three unseasonable
jests, than with the artful solution of the *fable*.[30] (pp. 313–314)

When discussing Jonson's and Congreve's theory and practice,
critics too often stress differences, which are peripheral, and slight
similarities, which are fundamental. A searching reappraisal of
Congreve's relation to Jonson in both theory and practice is an
essential prerequisite to a deeper and clearer understanding of
their respective achievements. The similarities between Congreve and Jonson are far more important for an understanding of
the ethical aspect of seventeenth-century comedy than are the
differences. Congreve's complete assimilation of and staunch adherence to the most idealistic convictions in Jonson's aesthetic
creed rings through the prologues, epilogues, and dedications of
Congreve's last two plays. Both dramatists, in defiance of popular
taste, held to an uncompromising belief in the validity of the dual
function of comedy—a principle stated by Aristotle and reiterated
by Horace. Each enunciates, although neither fully develops, a
theory of historic importance with which the dramatists' name
continues to be associated: Congreve, with the distinction between a witwoud and a truewit; Jonson with the distinction
between a humor and an affected humor. The creative process of
each is guided but seldom circumscribed by his theory; hence it
follows that the creative process of each may be traced with
greater perspicuity through a close analysis of his practice than by
a rigid application of his theory. A more thorough investigation of
the indebtedness of Etherege, Wycherley, Shadwell, and Congreve
to Jonson is long overdue. Once the extent and nature of their
response to Jonson's theory and practice has been determined, the
influence of the comedy of humors on the comedy of manners will
appear as formative and pervasive, and Congreve will emerge as
the last and most illustrious of the Sons of Ben.

NOTES

1 Henry Ten Eyck Perry, *The Comic Spirit in Restoration Drama* (New Haven, 1925), p. 79.

2 *A History of Restoration Comedy, 1660–1700* (Cambridge, Eng., 1923).

3 William Congreve, *Plays*, ed. Alexander C. Ewald (London, 1887). In citations from the plays of Jonson and Congreve we quote from the Mermaid Series, since it is adequate for our purposes and readily accessible.

4 In Jonson's *Epicoene*, Truewit warns Morose that wedlock frequently is a trap, that a worldly bride often chooses to convey her chastity to a "friend" before marriage just as "wise widows" transfer their estates: "... whom you are to marry, may have made a conveyance of her virginity aforehand, as your wise widows do of their [e]states, before they marry, in trust to some friend, sir ... and antedate you cuckold" (III [Act II, Scene 1], 172).

5 George Meredith, *An Essay on Comedy*, ed. Lane Cooper (New York, 1956), p. 97.—Meredith, frequently subtle and acute, errs here: "The comedy has no idea in it, beyond the stale one that so the world goes; and it concludes with the jaded discovery of a document at a convenient season for the descent of the curtain. A plot was an afterthought with Congreve ... His *Way of the World* might be called 'The Conquest of a Town Coquette'. ..."

6 The pursuit and surrender of Millamant is skillfully subordinated to the conflict between the pairs of adulterers; actually the witty couple appear alone together for approximately three pages in the park scene (II, 2), four and a half pages in the proviso scene (IV, 1), and exchange only five lines in the ensemble scene at the close of the play.

7 Thomas Davies, *Dramatic Miscellanies* (London, 1785), III, 386.

8 In Restoration comedy an eligible wit never voluntarily marries the woman who has granted him "the last favor"; Mrs. Fainall realizes the futility of demanding that Mirabell atone for having wronged her by becoming her husband.

9 *The Complete Works of William Congreve*, ed. Montague Summers (London, 1923), "Amendments to Mr. Collier's False and Imperfect Citations," III, 173. Hereafter cited as *Works*.

10 For other discussions of wit see: Thomas Fujimura, *The Restoration Comedy of Wit* (Princeton, 1952): Naturalism; John Harrington Smith, *The Gay Couple in Restoration Comedy* (Cambridge, Mass., 1948): Persiflage; Kathleen Lynch, *The Social Mode of Restoration Comedy* (New York, 1926): Preciosity.

11 *Works*, III, 163–64.

12 Origin and significance of the names: Truewit is the articulate, resourceful, and skeptical wit in Jonson's *Epicoene;* Witwoud is the most voluble, fanciful, and controversial false wit in Congreve's own last comedy.

    Because he appreciates the skill involved in portraying an affected wit, Davies (*Dramatic Miscellanies*, III, 378–379), makes one of the earliest and most penetrating comments on Witwoud's character: "To delineate the manners of a mere coxcomb, is not so difficult; but to give the picture of a man who incurs ridicule from the affectation of wit; one who says so many things like wit, that the common observer mistakes them for it, is not a cheap business: Witwoud cost the writer more pains than ten Tattles [false-wit in Congreve's *Love for Love*]."

13 *Works*, I, 94–96. All subsequent citations from Congreve's personal letters are from Vol. I.

14 Congreve's letter to Dennis, from Tunbridge-Wells, August 11, 1695, in *Works*, I, 95.

15 *Works*, I, 94.

16 *Works*, I, 70.

17 John Locke, *Essay Concerning Human Understanding* (Oxford, 1894), I, 204.

18 After Dennis suggests that "characters" of the company frequenting Tunbridge-Wells would be welcome, Congreve, ever reluctant to praise or blame and perhaps not too certain whether Dennis would regard publishable tidbits as confidential, replies: "… were the Company better, or worse, I would have you expect no Characters from me; for I profess myself an Enemy to Detraction; and who is there, that can justly merit Commendation?" (*Works*, I, 95).

19 In *Every Man in His Humour*, after Matthew, the plagiarizing poetaster, reads as his own a passage from "Hero and Leander," Edward Kno'well protests: "… he utters nothing but stolen remnants. … A filching rogue, hang him!—and from the dead! it's worse than sacrilege" (I [Act IV, Scene 1], 71–72).

20 The fallacies apparent in Leigh Hunt's indictment of "wit for wit's sake" arise from his own inability to assimilate Congreve's distinction between the character of a truewit and a witwoud. One of the sobering ironies of criticism is that here, unmindful of this distinction, Hunt censures the dramatist for having been the supreme exponent of the kind of false wit which Congreve himself so insistently and so brilliantly condemns. All too frequently generalizations on the nature and quality of Congreve's wit are still based on fallacious assumptions similar to or identical with those of Hunt: "But above all, we must confess we find the 'wit' become tiresome. We love it heartily in its proper places, in Butler, Swift, and Addison, where it is serving some purpose greater than itself. … But wit for wit's sake becomes a task and a trial; and in Congreve's days

it was a cant ... —as if all sense, and reason, and wit, had been comprised in the substitution of the greater faculties of man for the less, and the critical for the unconscious. Everybody was to be 'witty.' Letters were to be full of 'wit' and end in some 'witty turn.' Coffee-houses were to talk nothing but 'wit.' Ladies were to have 'wit and sweetness,' and gentlemen 'wit and fire'; not the old 'mother-wit' of Shakspeare and his fellows, which was a gift from the whole loving frame of Nature; but a trick of the fancy and of words, which you might almost acquire from the brother-wits of the tavern, and which dealt chiefly in simile, with a variation of antithesis. Every thing seemed to be of value, only inasmuch as it could be likened or opposed to something else; till at length simile and metaphor came to be taken for a 'reason;' and 'sense' itself was occupied, not in seeing into anything very deeply for its own sake, but in discovering how far it was capable of being split off into a couple of images. The great wits ... bantered the less, and affected to laugh at the affectation; but it was only for the purpose of guarding its rank and distinctions. This cant of wit ... came to its head in Congreve, and pretty well ceased with him" ("Biographical and Critical Notices," *Dramatic Works of Wycherley, Congreve, Van Brugh, and Farquhar*, ed. Leigh Hunt [London, 1866], p. xxx).

21 Congreve's letter to Dennis, August 11, 1695, in *Works*, I, 95.

22 "I made the plot as strong as I could, because it was single; and I made it single, because I would avoid confusion, ..."—("Epistle Dedicatory" to *The Double-Dealer*, pp. 98–99).

23 Gellert Spencer Alleman, *Matrimonial Law and the Materials of Restoration Comedy* (Wallingford, Penn., 1942), p. 33, discusses the realistic aspects of the masqued marriage: "... some of the situations which are absurd to us were not impossible or even improbable to a Restoration audience."

24 *Works*, III, 200.

25 Dedication to *The Mourning Bride*, p. 416.

26 *Works*, III, 202.

27 *The Comedy of Manners* (London, 1913), p. 192.

28 Ben Jonson, *Timber or Discoveries*, ed. Felix E. Schelling (Boston, 1892), pp. 81–82.

29 *Ibid.*, pp. 73–75.

30 *The Way of the World* and its dedication may be regarded as an indictment of the arrogant and gratuitous cynicism expressed in such plays as *Love's Last Shift* (1696), and its epilogue. Cibber's mercenary attitude toward playwriting is that of a huckster toward his wares—four acts of bawdry are admittedly designed for those whose taste runs to lewdness, a fifth act of lachrymose repentance for those more sentimentally inclined. Cibber's vulgarity, casuistry, and irresponsible juggling with values may have strengthened Congreve's desire to write a play which would reflect a knowledge of and a respect for the highest traditions of realistic comedy.